THE DAY OF THE LORD

Harrison Books by Bob Yandian

The Day of the Lord: What the Book of Joel Reveals About the Last Days and the Outpouring of the Spirit

Acts: A New Testament Commentary

Romans: A New Testament Commentary

Galatians: A New Testament Commentary

Ephesians: A New Testament Commentary

Philippians: A New Testament Commentary

Colossians: A New Testament Commentary

1 and 2 Thessalonians: A New Testament Commentary

Hebrews: A New Testament Commentary

James: A New Testament Commentary

Epistles of John: A New Testament Commentary

Proverbs: The Principles of Wisdom

Theology Simplified: The 8 Foundational Truths of Your Glorious Redemption

Theology Simplified, Volume 2: The Eight Foundational Truths for Understanding God's Plan for Man

The Grace of Healing: Revealing God's Heart to Heal

Leadership Secrets of David the King

Understanding the End Times

Calling and Separation

THE DAY OF THE LORD

What the Book of Joel Reveals About the Last Days and the Outpouring of the Spirit

BOB YANDIAN

All emphasis within Scripture quotations is the author's own.

Published by Harrison House Publishers
Shippensburg, PA 17257

ISBN 13 TP: 978-1-6675-1484-0
ISBN 13 eBook: 978-1-6675-1485-7

For Worldwide Distribution, Printed in the U.S.A.
1 2 3 4 5 6 7 8 / 30 29 28 27 26

CONTENTS

FOREWORD
BY RICK RENNER

Nearly four decades ago when my teaching ministry was just getting started, Pastor Bob Yandian was a source of tremendous encouragement to me. As I was launching out by faith to write my first book, he offered to write the foreword for it, and I will be forever grateful for his relationship with me and our family and for the way he constantly encouraged us. He blessed us with his counsel not only when we were first getting started in our U.S. ministry, but also when our family packed up and moved to the lands of the USSR. Now it's nearly four decades later, and we've seen God do so much. Pastor Bob was there to help us get started, and, now, to think that I am writing a foreword for one of his books — it is a great honor for me.

When Pastor Bob asked me to review this book and write a foreword for it, I did not realize how much it would impact me. However, I just finished reading this wonderful book, and I see it as one of the most precise, to the point, and comprehensive books I've ever read on prophetic subjects as they pertain to the past, present, and future. I've been a serious student of the Bible my whole life, but while reading this book, I learned things that I've never read or studied before, and Bob Yandian as a consummate teacher has marvelously laid it all out in a way that anyone can understand it.

I am completely captivated by how Pastor Bob has so well explained the insect invasion that is described by the prophet Joel — that is, the palmerworm, locust, cankerworm, and caterpillar. I've always longed for someone to really explain the prophetic meaning of these insects, and Bob has done it! He has delved deeply into cycles of judgment — a subject that alone is worth the entire book. But Bob has unwrapped the meaning of these insects in a way that has satisfied my heart's yearning, and these truths have application to every Christian's life. What he explains about these cycles of judgment is so powerful that I wish every Christian would read it to understand it.

But that is just the beginning...Pastor Bob then proceeds to cover a broad range of other events that include the coming of the Antichrist, the Battle of Armageddon, the future worldwide outpouring of the Holy Spirit, and the Millennial reign of Christ. To be honest, I am awed by how Bob has so compellingly covered these subjects. The fact is, he has opened the Book of Joel in a way that is so easy to understand for anyone with a heart to learn. Beginning with the first chapter of Joel and continuing to the last, he opens prophetic scriptures and reveals to our eyes where we are today and what is coming in the near future. *To say it is thrilling is an understatement.* I truly believe what you find in this book will hold your attention and that it will answer many of your questions about our current age and the one to come.

Pastor Bob, I wish to thank you for opening the Book of Joel to me in this remarkable way. I am especially thankful for your commentary on the meaning of repentance and about the last great outpouring of the Holy Spirit and how it will transform the world when it occurs. As I read that portion of this book, my heart rejoiced to think of the moment when we will see that last-days worldwide visitation, which, as you teach, is in the days before us.

As a lover of God's Word and a friend who is grateful to Pastor Bob for his input in my own life — and for his years of seasoned ministry that have been filled with integrity — I am thankful to come alongside him to heartily endorse this book and to write this foreword. I boldly encourage you to read this book from beginning to end with the expectation that God will open your spiritual eyes to many profound truths. Know that the truths you are about to read are coming to you from the spirit, mind, and hand of a man whom God has trusted, and is still trusting, to bring the Body of Christ rich teachings from His Word that are trustworthy.

Now...it's time for you to dive into this book and to prepare your heart to receive illumination from God concerning things past, present, and future — and a glorious and hopeful look into what His Spirit will do in the days to come!

Rick Renner

Minister, Author, Broadcaster

Moscow, Russia

1

CYCLES OF JUDGMENT

JOEL 1:1-5

1-5 "The word of the Lord that came to Joel the son of Pethuel. Hear this, you elders [leaders of the land], *and give ear, all you inhabitants of the land! Has anything like this happened in your days, or even in the days of your fathers?*

Tell your children about it, let your children tell their children, and their children another generation.

What the chewing locust [palmerworm KJV] left, the swarming locust has eaten; what the swarming locust left, the crawling locust [cankerworm KJV] has eaten; and what the crawling locust left, the consuming locust [caterpillar KJV] has eaten.

Awake you drunkards and weep; and wail all you drinkers of wine, because of the new wine, for it has been cut off from your mouth.

The Time of Joel's Book

Joel wrote his book during a time of apostasy, described in verse 5. The nation was spending its time drinking and in drunkenness. The people of God were trying to substitute the presence and friendship of the Holy Spirit with natural things. They were obsessed with the world's comforts and ignoring God's Word and power. In essence, carnality was the spiritual condition of the believers of Israel.

What had happened to the nation of Israel to cause this falling away from Jehovah? Very simply, they had become accustomed to prosperity. Of course, there is nothing wrong with prosperity. It is a biblical truth and blessing in both the Old and New Testaments. I believe it and I teach it. But like all biblical issues, there can be an abuse of any of God's blessings. Grace is another example today, one blessing of God used for carnality. "...Shall we continue in sin so grace may abound? Certainly not!..." (Romans 6:1-2).

With all prosperity comes warnings. The danger is, you can get your eyes and dependency off the Lord and onto your money. The Bible does not teach that money is the root of all evil. It teaches the love of money is the root of all evil. You do not even have to have money to have the love of it. When you begin to love money, you become a servant to it. Your fear of losing it drives your decisions. Money makes a great servant, but a terrible master.

Much of Israel's History Revolved Around Money

Why did the children of Israel eventually lose favor with God after they had conquered Canaan? There was the original generation that the Lord had led out of the bondage of Egypt. They came into the wilderness where, as the old saying goes, "God got them out of Egypt, but He couldn't get Egypt out of them." They eventually died in the wilderness. But the next generation went across into Canaan and became one of the wealthiest generations in Israel's history.

God called them to go in and take over the Promised Land, which they did. They defeated their enemies and took the spoils of war from the different cities they conquered and inhabited. But by the time the book of Joshua ended, we find them sitting down. They no longer wanted to conquer. They just wanted to sit on their new sofas and enjoy their luxuries. Now luxuries are nice and should be enjoyed. But not at the expense of your relationship with God. And that is exactly what happened.

By the time of the prophet Joel, the nation of Israel was enjoying tremendous prosperity, but the salt within the nation was losing its savor, believers were becoming carnal, lovers of pleasure more than lovers of God (2 Timothy 3:1-5). Fault is laid at the feet of the elders, the spiritual leaders of the nation. They had not been instructing people in the Word of God. Their failure to teach the scriptures had resulted in the nation's carnality and self-indulgent attitude. The nation was spending its time and energy in the pursuit of pleasure, in drinking and partying. Drinking wine and liquor was the chief preoccupation of the people. Even the priests, the spiritual leaders, were getting drunk. Later, a terrible plague came against the nation.

THE MAN, HIS TIME OF MINISTRY, AND ISRAEL'S CONDITION

Joel is one of the prophets of the Old Testament. He wrote before the Babylonian captivity, the 70-year period when the children of Israel were taken captive by the armies of Babylon.

Joel's father's name, *Pethuel,* means "persuaded of God." Joel came from a seemingly godly family, and his parents were not afraid to name him with a spiritual calling.

Joel's day was a momentary wake-up call in Israel's history. Until this time the Jews turned against God and were quick to worship idols. They were always inquisitive and fascinated by false religions. But after their return from captivity in Babylon, they never returned to idols again. Before Babylon, perversions were the norm; sexual sin and immorality was rampant in the nation.

But after the Babylonian captivity, the nation repented, turned back to God, and His Word became their standard for daily life. As a result, Israel enjoyed one of the greatest times of prosperity in its entire history. The golden years of Israel lasted more than 400 years. During this time, the children of Israel literally fulfilled the blessings of Deuteronomy 28. They were blessed coming in and going out, the city and in the field, in their flocks and herds; everything they put their hand to prospered. The Lord made them plenteous in goods. They were lenders to many nations and borrowed from no one. Other nations came to Israel to borrow from them, and Israel became a banking nation for the nations.

But then a terrible thing happened. Israel became *religious.* They turned from following faith in God to becoming followers of the law. They were highly moral, without God's power. They substituted their moral works for faith in God's grace. They were intent on observing every detail of the law. But there was something very wrong. They did all this in an attempt to merit the blessings of God. And on his own, no one can ever merit the least of God's blessings.

The nation of Israel became extremely religious. They turned the law into a means of salvation, almost worshipping it, which was exactly the situation that existed at the time of Jesus' first coming. He came into a nation bound by religion.

They even added laws to the law to keep people further away from sinning against the Law of Moses. Jesus and Paul both called these *traditions* of men. Jesus was not afraid to break their traditions but never broke God's Word.

Religious people are the hardest to win to true repentance and salvation. Religious people are proud. They do not understand that the need for salvation is for everyone because everyone is born in sin separated from the life of God. That new life they need does not come from our works because we have nothing to offer God. God only asks for faith in what He has done through the work of His Son, Jesus, on the Cross.

When Jesus entered into history, preaching throughout Palestine and winning over the multitudes, the Gospels say, "the common people heard Him gladly" (Mark 12:37).

Prostitutes and tax collectors came to Him freely. The only ones our Lord had a difficult time winning over were the religious leaders of His time, especially the Scribes and Pharisees. As far as we know only a few religious people of Jesus' day ever accepted Him as Savior. Yet, many thousands of common people, citizens from all nations, followed Him and His message. And multitudes of them made commitments to Him, accepting Him as their Messiah, their personal Savior and Lord.

At the time of Joel, the nation was filled with apathy toward godliness and apostasy toward God's Word. As it is with all sin, the nation was "lovers of self." Joel lived in the southern kingdom, Judah. He lived during the time of a devastating locust invasion. This is the background of the book. This devastating invasion of insects had already occurred by the time Joel wrote these words in verse 4. The insects he describes give an indication of the severity of the destruction that was wrought upon the Jewish nation. These will be used by Joel and the Holy Spirit to reveal Israel's national future and God's eventual plan for the nation.

The Plague

Four types of locusts invaded the land. In verse 4 they are called by four different names (I will use the KJV translation to name them). From the first to the fourth, the palmerworms, locusts, cankerworms, and caterpillars. All four are different types of locusts. Joel used the invasions to issue a warning and prophecy of the future of Israel to the people.

The prophets of the Old Testament usually took an event like this and used it to teach about coming events. Let me give you some examples.

Jonah was three days and three nights in the belly of the whale. Later, Jesus referred to this event (Matthew 12:39-41). What was Jonah's experience a type of? It was prophecy of our Lord's death, burial, and resurrection. "For as Jonah was three days and three nights in the belly of the great fish, so will the Son of Man be three days and three nights in the heart of the earth" (Matthew 12:40). What happened after the whale spit Jonah out on dry land? He went and preached to the Gentiles of Nineveh. When Jesus came out of "the heart of the earth," He turned to the Gentiles, beginning the Church Age, and sent disciples to the uttermost parts of the earth.

Jesus used Noah and the flood (Matthew 24:37-41) as a type of the transition from the end of the Tribulation to the beginning of the millennial reign of Jesus.

He used the Queen of Sheba as an example of a Gentile and a woman of the Old Testament who came searching for wisdom and found the Lord. She will stand on the side of righteousness in heaven at the Great White Throne Judgment (Matthew 12:42).

Jesus delighted telling of Gentiles of the Old Testament who had greater faith than the inhabitants of Israel at the time. He used the widow who fed Elijah and Naaman who was healed of leprosy under Elisha (Luke 4:25-27).

The Old Testament prophets were quoted quite often by Jesus and other disciples. Jesus quoted Daniel, Isaiah, Jeremiah, and others. And Joel, the prophet we are studying, was quoted by Peter on the day of Pentecost.

Standing in the middle of devastation like the citizens of Israel had never seen, Joel tells of four military invasions to come, which parallel the four invasions of insects they have witnessed. The first locust wave, the chewing locust (*gasam*, cutters) took the top of the stalk. The next (*arbah*, swarming) devoured the stalk itself. The third wave, the crawling locusts (*yeleg*, lick up) entered the land and ate the stubble off the ground. And the fourth and final wave, the consuming locusts (*chaciyl*, devouring) burrowed under the ground and ate the buried root.

There was no way in the natural mind this could be turned around and saved. Yet, just as God will save the nation of Israel, no matter how impossible and how much devastation has occurred, He will deliver His people, nation, and city—Jerusalem. He will also deliver His people, the Jews, in the midst of overwhelming military and satanic odds.

The message of Joel is the same message to us today in our personal problems and in those of our nation and world. We must take our eyes off our problems, no matter how devastating they seem, and turn them back onto the promises of God. The problems of our life and generation are temporary. God's answers are eternal. No natural problem can change eternal answers. But eternal answers can change natural problems.

Even Your Problems Can Be Teachers

What Joel was telling the people was, "This is a historic moment. You are looking at something that has never happened to your fathers or your fathers' fathers before them. Hear and listen; look at what has happened." Then he adds, "Learn a lesson from it and teach it to your children."

We can learn great lessons during our times of blessing. But we can learn even greater lessons during our times of adversity. Jesus, Paul, Peter, James, and John told us we would have difficult times during our Christian life. But our answer from Jesus is, "be of good cheer, I have overcome the world" (John 16:33). We are given weapons to use against our enemy. This tells us we are going to have seasons of attack from Satan, but God has already prepared weapons for us superior to our adversary. We can withstand and win in the evil day of attack (Ephesians 6:10-17). We can learn when times are good, and we can learn when times are bad.

Famine Is a Time for Reexamination and a Return to Faith

God chose this time of famine to exhort the people in Joel's day to learn from their dreadful experience. If God can deliver Israel from its greatest time of trouble yet to come, He can and will deliver them from their present distress. Israel's history to this point includes deliverance from greater things than locusts and famine. He kept them through 400 years of slavery, brought them through the Red Sea, been faithful to them through 40 years in the desert, crossing the Jordan River, and victory over all the cities of Canaan. What is a famine to the God of creation and Redeemer from the destruction?

Joel is so assured God will deliver the people he is ministering to, he tells them to tell of God's deliverance to their children, their grandchildren, and all their children afterward. Joel is assuring them ahead of time they will survive this famine and tell future generations of God's delivering power.

The Four Coming Invasions

The book of Joel was written some time between 830 and 800 BC during the reign of King Joash of Judah. Throughout the book, the northern kingdom of Samaria is not mentioned. Apparently the book was written after the defeat of the northern kingdom. These four invasions are yet to come, showing the authenticity of Joel's book and the accuracy of the prophet to hear the voice of the Holy Spirit.

The first military invasion will be Assyria. Like the first swarm of locusts that took the fruit off the top of the stalks, Assyria will take the wealth of Israel. This one invasion will be made up of four separate attacks under four different Assyrian kings.

The second invasion will be from the Babylonians. They will come for the stalk and what wealth the nation possesses at the time. Israel will become a wasteland after this invasion and the temple will be robbed and demolished. The Jewish people will be killed, starved and the survivors enslaved in Babylon for 70 years. Isaiah and Jeremiah will prophesy of its coming and Daniel will be raised up during the Babylonian enslavement to tell of Israel's time and God's method of coming deliverance.

The third invasion will occur during the time of the reign of the Roman Empire and after the day of Pentecost. This invasion will occur in AD 70 and the Roman army will destroy Jerusalem and demolish and burn the temple. Outside the temple, Jesus told His disciples this was coming (Matthew 24:2; Luke 21:20-24). Like the removal of the stubble, no remaining evidence of Israel's existence will be seen for more than 2,000 years.

The fourth invasion is yet to come and possibly in our day. It will involve all the nations of the world under the control of the antichrist, coming in unity to destroy Jerusalem, Israel and its temple. This is the battle of Armageddon.

This one event, Armageddon, will be the major subject of Joel and will occupy Chapters 2 and 3 of this book. Armageddon will be the only battle given in detail. The first three are not given individually, but the aftermath of these battles, and their result on the land, will occupy the remainder of Chapter 1.

God already foretold of Satan's fall and his present control over the nations. He also has foretold of Satan's defeat and removal from the earth. This is not only told in the New Testament, but also the Old. This is why Joel could be so confident Israel would remain forever. He told the Israelites that one day they would tell their children, grandchildren, and great grandchildren of God's victory. The prophecies of the Old Testament, even though written of events to take place *in that day*, relate to generations yet to come until the final return of the Lord Jesus to rule the earth. If Joel's generation could be sure of God's deliverance in their life, we also can read Joel, knowing it speaks of our deliverance today.

What has Joel spoken to our time period? The answer is found in Joel chapter 2 where the Lord tells us, "And it shall come to pass afterward that I will pour out My Spirit on all flesh; your sons and your daughters shall prophesy, your old men shall dream dreams, your young men shall see visions. And also on My menservants and on My maidservants I will pour out My Spirit in those days" (Joel 2:28-29).

Peter used this verse on the Day of Pentecost when the Church began. Although Joel meant it for the day of the beginning of Jesus' rule on earth through the newly formed Church at Pentecost. Old Testament prophets spoke specifically to their generation of certain events near and distant, but their words apply to all people in all time periods. Joel's writings are also quoted by Amos (1:2; 9:13) and Isaiah (13:6). The Word of God is timeless.

A Broad Vision of Joel's Prophecy

The first five verses tell of four locust invasions that will occur after the writing of the book. Joel used these events as an object lesson. Through it he warned the people to turn back to the Lord. He also used it to foretell a future occurrence of far greater significance to all future generations. This is why he encouraged the people to repeat his words to their offspring then to be retold for generations to come. Their survival comes with a solemn warning to prepare each generation after them in God's Word.

Then in verses 6 through 14, Joel compares these insect invasions to a future event that is going to come to pass one generation after Joel is gone, the invasion of the Assyrians. Then there will be three other invasions ending at the return of Jesus to rule the earth. Each wave is compared to the types of locusts that invaded the land. Each wave is going to be more devastating than the one before it, until the fourth and last one that almost destroys Israel at Armageddon. Only a divine intervention by Jesus Himself will spare Israel and Jerusalem.

Now, answer carefully. Did Israel survive the locust invasion? Yes. Did Israel survive the attacks of Assyria? Yes. We know this from history. We also know it because we know that God established the nation of Israel to last forever. Therefore, since Israel survived the attack of the locusts and since they survived the attack of the Assyrians, we can be assured they are going to survive the battle of Armageddon! Because the same Lord who delivered them from the pestilence and from the Assyrian hordes is the same Lord who has promised to deliver them even during the Great Tribulation. "He who endures to the end [of the Tribulation] shall be saved [spared]" (Matthew

24:13). God gives information in Matthew and Revelation how the saved Jews of the Tribulation can enter the worldwide millennial reign of Jesus Christ.

Jesus is the same Lord we trust in today for our salvation and deliverance. Whether it is physical circumstances or spiritual battles we go through, the Lord can deliver us out of them *all.*

Sin and God's Protection

In the Old Testament book of Leviticus we see five progressive cycles a nation goes through as it rejects the Lord's authority. I use the term *cycles* for a reason. There are five levels of protection that God can exercise over those who put their trust in Him. As one turns away from God into sin, step by step he removes himself from God's protective care and exposes himself to successively destructive attacks by the enemy.

Let me illustrate by using myself as an example. If I sinned and did not confess it, that unconfessed sin might bring a catastrophe into my life. Yet, God would not allow me to be completely destroyed by it. But the longer I remained in sin, excusing my lack of obedience to God, the deeper I would be drawn into its web. The more I persisted in living in spiritual rebellion against God, the more His protective shield over me would be withdrawn.

Finally, there would be no divine protection around me at all. No defense against the attacks of Satan. At that moment, the enemy could have free rein to come in and totally destroy me. And not because God failed to protect me, but because I failed to keep myself positioned under His shield of protection.

Gradually, step by step, I would have removed myself from the secret place of the Most High and from the under the shadow of the Almighty, exposing myself to the attacks of the enemy. Although Satan could not steal my salvation, he could rob my health, income, and reputation in my community. I might die early under the sin unto death (1 Corinthians 5:5), and Jesus would meet me at heaven's gate saying, "Stupid, stupid, stupid."

It is for nations as well as individuals God has levels of protection, degrees of defense that He can provide based on our attitudes and actions. In Leviticus 26, we find that there are five cycles of judgment for those who draw themselves away from God's divine protection by engaging in sin. Each of these five stages is progressively worse than the one before. In fact, each is declared by the scriptures to be seven times worse than the judgments that preceded it.

But the Bible also points out that in each case, if the individual or nation will turn back to Him, God will stop the judgments. But without repentance, God cannot stop these judgments from falling, whether upon an individual or a nation of people.

The Five Cycles of Judgment

Cycle 1

The first cycle of judgment is *sickness*. It is described in Leviticus 26:14-17: "But if you do not obey Me, and do not observe all these commandments, and if you despise My statutes, or if your soul abhors My judgments, so that you do not perform all My commandments but break My covenant, I also will do this to you: I will even appoint terror over you, wasting disease and fever which shall consume the eyes and cause sorrow of heart. And you shall sow your seed in vain, for your enemies shall eat it. I will set My face against you, and you shall be defeated by your enemies. Those who hate you shall reign over you, and you shall flee when no one pursues you."

This first cycle has to do with terror, extreme fear. Proverbs 28:1 says, "The wicked flee when no one pursues." Why? Terror is usually exaggerated fear. It has no source but our own imagination. It is proven by research in our own day that more than 70 percent of what we fear never comes to pass. We often spend money to protect ourselves from what is too bad to be true and invest money into what is too good to be true. Both are based on exaggerated fear.

In the New Testament, the apostle Paul tells us as Christians, "For God has not given us a spirit of fear, but of power and of love and of a sound mind" (2 Timothy 1:7). That is good news. Why? Because fear produces sickness, mental and physical. When a person begins to walk in sin, illness, of one kind or another, will attach itself to his body. The first cycle of judgment is *sickness*.

Cycle 2

The second cycle of judgment is *crop failure*. This is found in Leviticus 26:18-20: "And after all this, if you do not obey Me, then I will punish you seven times more for your sins. I will break the pride of your power; I will make your heavens like iron and your earth like bronze. And your strength shall be spent in vain; for your land shall not yield its produce, nor shall the trees of the land yield their fruit."

Stop and examine these verses for a moment. Where does Joel and his prophecy fit into all this? By the time of Joel's writing, the people of Israel had already gone past the first cycle and had entered the second. They had already progressed from physical illness to the failure of their agricultural production. They were experiencing the anguish of famine, that terrible time when the heavens become as iron and the earth as brass. When the invaders come in to steal the crops and the land no longer yields its harvest.

Cycle 3

The third cycle of judgment is *destruction of children and animals*. This is described in Leviticus 26:21-22: "Then, if you walk contrary to Me, and are not willing to obey Me, I will bring on you seven times more plagues, according to your sins. I will also send wild beasts among you, which shall rob you of your children, destroy your livestock, and make you few in number; and your highways shall be desolate."

According to Leviticus 26:22, *wild beasts* (terrorist attackers) will come in to ravage the nation to kill the innocent children and the young of the flocks and herds. As a result, the inhabitants of the land will decrease in number and in ability to provide for their growing physical needs.

Cycle 4

The fourth cycle of judgment is *military occupation*. This is described in Leviticus 26:23-26:

> And if by these things you are not reformed by Me, but walk contrary to Me, then I also will walk contrary

> to you, and I will punish you yet seven times for your sins. And I will bring a sword against you that will execute the vengeance of the covenant; when you are gathered together within your cities I will send pestilence among you; and you shall be delivered into the hand of the enemy. When I have cut off your supply of bread, ten women shall bake your bread in one oven, and they shall bring back your bread by weight, and you shall eat and not be satisfied.

The sinning nation will be overrun and controlled by an outside power. Another nation will come in to take over the land. The people will still be allowed to remain in their own country, but they will come under domination by a foreign government. A military dictatorship will be imposed upon them. The controlling nation will eat well and be comfortable, but the servant nation will always be hungry or not have enough of life's necessities.

When Jesus was born on earth, Israel was under the fourth cycle of judgment. They were controlled by Rome. They had already gone through the first three cycles and were in cycle four. Their once proud and powerful nation had been reduced to nothing more than a minor province under the mighty and pagan power of the Roman Empire.

Cycle 5

The fifth and final judgment is *destruction, captivity and enslavement in a foreign land* as described in Leviticus 26:27-39:

And after all this, if you do not obey Me, but walk contrary to Me, then I also will walk contrary to you in fury; and I, even I, will chastise you seven times for your sins. You shall eat the flesh of your sons, and you shall eat the flesh of your daughters. I will destroy your high places, cut down your incense altars, and cast your carcasses on the lifeless forms of your idols; and My soul shall abhor you.

I will lay your cities waste and bring your sanctuaries to desolation, and I will not smell the fragrance of your sweet aromas. I will bring the land to desolation, and your enemies who dwell in it shall be astonished at it. I will scatter you among the nations and draw out a sword after you; your land shall be desolate and your cities waste.

Then the land shall enjoy its sabbaths as long as it lies desolate and you are in your enemies' land; then the land shall rest and enjoy its sabbaths. As long as it lies desolate it shall rest—for the time it did not rest on your sabbaths when you dwelt in it.

And as for those of you who are left, I will send faintness into their hearts in the lands of their enemies; the sound of a shaken leaf shall cause them to flee; they shall flee as though fleeing from a sword, and they shall fall when no one pursues.

They shall stumble over one another, as it were before a sword, when no one pursues; and you shall have no power to stand before your enemies.

You shall perish among the nations, and the land of your enemies shall eat you up. And those of you

> who are left shall waste away in their iniquity in your enemies' lands; also in their fathers' iniquities, which are with them, they shall waste away.

This has happened twice to the nation of Israel. It happened once when they were overrun, captured, and carried off to Babylon. At that time their city was destroyed and their people taken away as many were killed and others taken captive. For 70 years they were held as slaves in a heathen land. After that time, a remnant did come back to Israel and take possession of the land to rebuild Israel and Jerusalem.

That return was the end of that cycle. Today the nation of Israel is under the fifth cycle of judgment again and will be until Jesus returns. Yes, we see the Jews returning to the Promised Land today. But the majority of that nation is still scattered around the world and has been since the time of the Lord Jesus Christ.

Jesus entered this earth while the nation of Israel was in its fourth cycle of judgment. They were still under foreign dominion, Rome, at the time of Christ. But then because they rejected their God-sent Messiah, they entered into the fifth cycle of judgment. The city of Jerusalem was overrun, the temple demolished, and the nation of Israel taken away into captivity and scattered across the face of the entire world. That situation has not changed to this day. The people of Israel have been dispersed throughout the world now for almost 2,000 years. But God still keeps His word. They are going to return in total to that nation, and it will come to its full climax when Jesus returns to establish His kingdom on earth.

The closing verses of Leviticus 26:40-46 tell us that even after five cycles of judgment, God will still be open to the repentance of His people and will turn their situation around. That event will come at the end of the Tribulation, just before Jesus returns to rescue Israel and Jerusalem from the forces and captivity of other nations. He will restore the nation of Israel to a greater glory than ever—and Jerusalem to the eternal throne of Jesus Christ forever. The saved from all generations and nations will occupy the earth and visit the city of Jerusalem to see Jesus.

God's Challenge to Joel's Generation to Wake Up

> 1:5 "Awake you drunkards, and weep; and wail all you drinkers of wine, because of the new wine, for it has been cut off from your mouth."

We return to the fifth verse of Joel chapter 1. As we have seen, at the time of Joel, Israel was in cycle two of its judgment. They were experiencing crop failure. In the fifth and final verse of this section, Joel addresses the drunkards of the nation, rebuking and warning them because of their excessive drinking. Why? What does Joel's remarks about *drinking* have to do with Israel's present failure and future situation?

What is wine made of? Grapes. What is liquor made of? Grain. Where do grapes and grain come from? The crops of the field. What happened to the crops? They have been wiped from sight by the invading hordes of insects. What will happen to all those people who have been sitting back enjoying their prosperity and getting drunk? Joel tells them, "You can begin to weep and howl now because your source of *spirits* has just been cut *off!* Now where will you turn for comfort and enjoyment?" When natural "crutches" are removed, a person has to look for another.

God does not like it when His people, Israel, or the Church, turn from His presence, His Word, and His Holy Spirit to find something corruptible to lean on. God's Word, which is more than a crutch, is a stabilizer that cannot be removed or destroyed. Why look to the world or what it offers for stability. The world and everything it has to offer is temporary. Only God's words live and abides forever. "Heaven and earth will pass away, but My words will by no means pass away" (Matthew 24:35).

The purpose of this book is not to argue the scriptural views of drinking wine, but the issue of, *what are you leaning on in your life?* Is your trust in corruptible things offered by the world or the incorruptible, eternal Word, and presence of God?

THE NEW WINE OF GOD'S HOLY SPIRIT

With this word, Joel not only points out the judgment that has fallen on the children of Israel because of their rejection of their God, he also begins his prophetic word that applies to every generation to come. For now begins one of the basic themes of the book of Joel: the fact that the Messiah is coming to provide a new type of wine. A new kind of *spirit*. A "wine that makes glad the heart of man" (Psalm 104:15). A wine that does not come from man and can never be taken away. No devastation can destroy it, no enemy can steal it, no demon in hell can spoil it. For this new wine is *the wine of the Holy Spirit of God.*

Joel tells of the day when that wine will be poured universally on all saved flesh. You and I are living in its early days right now. It began on the Day of Pentecost and never ended. But it will reach its full climax at the time of the millennial reign of the Lord Jesus Christ. In that day all the world's population will be able to live and enjoy all the fullness of this forever new wine.

The apostle Paul summarized the message of Joel when he compared placing our life's dependence on the natural, changeable objects of life to the spiritual and unchangeable gifts of God. It is like natural wine compared to the heavenly wine of the Holy Spirit. "Do not be drunk [overtaken] with [natural] wine, in which is dissipation [in excess]; but be filled [continually] with the [Holy] Spirit" (Ephesians 5:18).

This new wine is made available to us freely through Jesus Christ our Lord!

2

THE INVASION OF THE ASSYRIANS

JOEL 1:6-14

In Chapter 1 and in the Scripture passage Joel 1:1-5, we studied the four invasions of the locusts. Now in verses 6-14 we will see how Joel compares the first locust invasion to the coming invasion by the Assyrians.

The reason Israel will fall to the Assyrians is because the leadership of the nation, the *spiritual* leadership, will have degenerated. The spiritual leaders of the nation were no longer obeying the Lord. And, as has been said, *as goes the spiritual leaders, so goes the nation.* Judgment will fall on Israel for the same reason it falls on any nation that is supposed to be dedicated to God. The believers, the salt in the nation, loses its savor, its ability to preserve the nation.

The cause for judgment in Joel's book is the believers in Israel. And the first place the judgment is going to strike is on those most responsible for the spiritual climate of the nation, the priests and ministers of the people. They are charged with temple worship. Those whose duty it is to act as intermediaries between God and His people. From there, judgment is directed toward the believers throughout all levels of society. This is why Joel issues a rebuke to priests and the people alike who have forsaken the worship and service of the Lord to engage in the endless pursuits of selfish pleasure. Joel warns them of the impending disaster that is about to fall on them from outside their borders.

Four Assyrian Kings

> 1:6 "For a nation has come up against My land, strong, and without number; his teeth are the teeth of a lion, and he has the fangs of a fierce lion."

With this verse, Joel steps into future prophecy. The nation who is going to invade Israel will be Assyria. The full attack will be accomplished in four waves, four separate attacks, under four kings.

Who Is Assyria?

The Assyrian invasion is described in Isaiah chapters 7 through 11. We learn from these verses interesting facts about their invading power. Assyria had no right to be a strong nation. It was one of the most peculiar nations in the ancient world. It had no natural defenses. No surrounding mountain ranges to shield it from invasion as many other nations had, including Israel. One of the reasons Israel was so successful in repelling invasions throughout its history was because of its fortunate geographic location, being protected by natural barriers, mountains surrounding it on all but one side. There is only one break in Israel's natural defense perimeter, an opening on the north side.

I have visited the Holy Land and remember well the mountainous terrain that surrounds Israel on all sides except the north where a natural plain leads all the way up to Russia. Most Bible scholars believe it will be through this natural corridor that Russia will one day march on Israel (Ezekiel 38–39).

But Assyria was a very different land. By all accounts because of its small size, limited natural resources, and unprotected location, it should not have been a strong nation. Yet, despite all these drawbacks the Assyrians built a strong political and military power that was able to overrun and conquer many of the surrounding nations.

Four Assyrian Kings Attack Israel

In Isaiah chapters 7 through 11, we are introduced to the first of four kings who would rise up to attack and eventually conquer Israel. This king is symbolized in Joel 1:4 as the first wave of locusts, stripping the tops of the crops and claiming the choicest fruits of the land—representing the spoils of conquest. He took from Israel its finest treasures, including gold and silver. His name was Tiglath-Pileser, also known as Pul, as mentioned in Isaiah 66:19.

Tiglath-Pileser has a very interesting background. He was a gardener for the Assyrian king. Each day he would look through the garden windows into the king's place where court was being held. Realizing that the reigning monarch was not at all gifted in state affairs, he decided he could rule the nation better. So he personally assassinated the king, setting himself on the throne. As a gifted administrator, it was not long before he reorganized the government, rebuilt the military, and launched the nation on a series of highly successful military campaigns aimed at fully taking over the known world at that time.

The next three kings continued the military conquests of surrounding nations. All three individually, like Tiglath-Pileser, attacked Israel. The next king was Sargon II, who took the throne after Tiglath-Pileser. His story is found in Isaiah chapter 20. He also came through Israel after Tiglath-Pileser, and he further destroyed the nation his predecessor had begun to conquer.

The third king, the one with whom we are most familiar is Sennacherib. He came against Israel in the time of Hezekiah the king, and 185,000 of his army was destroyed in one night by Jesus Christ Himself—the Angel of the Lord. His story is found 2 Kings 18, Psalm 46, and Isaiah 36–39.

Finally, the fourth king was Esarhaddon, the son of Sennacherib. His name is mentioned in 2 Kings 19:37, Ezra 4:2, and Isaiah 37:38.

The Assyrian Attack

> 1:6 "For a nation has come up against My land, strong, and without number; his teeth are the teeth of a lion, and he has the fangs of a fierce lion."

Just like the locusts that invaded the land of Israel, according to Joel there was to come an army so vast across the land the natural eye could not number it. In fact, in Psalm 46 written by Hezekiah, he describes the scene before Jerusalem when it was surrounded by the numberless armies of the Assyrians, comparing it to an ocean moving in and surrounding the mountains. That is exactly what it looked like to King Hezekiah when Sennacherib's army came pouring in to attack Jerusalem. It looked like a moving sea of men, horses, and weapons.

This is how Joel describes the nation of Assyria as it came against Israel: he saw it as vast in number and having weapons as the teeth of fierce lions.

The first "teeth" mentioned here are the front teeth. The next "teeth" are the "cheek teeth," or the jaw teeth. What is the difference between your front teeth and your jaw teeth? The front ones are for biting. The back ones are for chewing. So, this invading nation is not only going to come in and bite, but they will also chew up and devour. This military attack is compared to the locust invasion, the biting and devouring swarms of insects.

The Assyrians will have no concern for human life or decency. They will have no mercy, no pity, no regard for property or life—whether man, woman, or child. They will come in to devastate and ravage the country from one end to the other. Their mission is to loot and plunder, pillage and burn, destroy the men, rape the women, and slay the children.

This is exactly what happens when a nation comes to take over another for only one reason: domination. This will happen again to Israel when Babylon attacks in 586 BC, and Rome attacks and destroys Israel and Jerusalem in AD 70. The only difference with the attack by Rome, Jerusalem will not only be destroyed and plundered—but the people will also be scattered into the other nations of the world for over 2,000 years after this battle. Then centuries later, Israel will be reestablished again as the home of the Jewish nation with Jerusalem as its capital.

THE TREE OF ISRAEL

> 1:7 "He has laid waste My vine and ruined My fig tree; he has stripped it bare and thrown it away; its branches are made white."

"He has laid waste My vine...." When the Lord says *My vine*, He is not particularly referring to the nation of Israel. He is talking about the believers *in* the nation. When the devourer came through the land of Israel, not only did he destroy the sinners, but he also destroyed the believers as well. Why was he able to destroy the righteous along with the unrighteous? Because they were as carnal as the unbelievers. They were all asleep spiritually—and not only asleep, but drunk. Priests and citizens alike were both truly fulfilling verse 5, which spoke of the drunkenness and corruption of the nation.

The spiritual leadership of Israel became so accustomed to prosperity they turned their eyes away from the Lord and were using God's blessings for sin. They were warned about this corruption, but in their headlong pursuit of selfish pleasure, they did not heed God's repeated warnings of coming invasion and national judgment.

When the hordes of locusts came in and destroyed everything before them, God's spokesman, Joel, raised some troubling questions. Why did this happen? How could the enemy gain entrance and bring such devastation upon God's very own people? The answer is simple: it happened because of the spiritual condition of the people of the land.

There is a lesson here for us in our generation. Many times disaster in the life of the individual Christian—as in the life of a nation—can be directly traced back to the spiritual condition of that person or people. As goes the spiritual life, so goes the natural life. Your spiritual life is a rudder for your natural life.

That is not meant to be a blanket judgment or condemnation. I am not saying that every believer who experiences trouble in their lives has brought the trouble upon themselves because they are living in sin. I realize that attacks on Christians arise for many different reasons. The truth is, trouble comes upon those who do right just as it comes on those who do wrong. Disaster is not automatically a sign of a lack of spirituality.

But what I am saying is: without a strong spiritual foundation and commitment, and a vital and active faith, the believer has no hope of warding off these attacks of the enemy—especially if the believer is engaging in sin and is too proud or stubborn to admit it and turn from the sin. God will not protect those who are unwise and will not seek His protective care. He also cannot protect those who refuse to remain under His protection.

If any nation is to live in security, the believers within that society must be careful not to let down their spiritual standard. They are the salt—the spiritual protector of the land. Today, God is demanding and expecting more personal commitment from His Church. That is why it is so important that we read and understand the Word of God, including His message to us here in the book of Joel.

Because the children of Israel let down their standard—because they did not render unto the Lord what rightfully belonged to Him—they opened themselves to attack from their enemy. And, as the Lord warned, they reaped what they had sown. They had no one to blame for their destruction but themselves.

I believe we as a generation need to take more responsibility for what God has taught us, shown us, and given to us in His grace. God never blesses without demanding we use those blessings to spread His gospel and His Word. The Great Commission to preach the gospel and make disciples has been given to all generations. We should not only be concerned about our own country but about other nations also. The gospel is to be carried to all the world. Why does God desire to prosper His people? So we, as the body of Christ, can send finances to other nations to help equip the Christians there, to preach the gospel, to create converts, and make disciples of them.

Along with this outpouring of His Spirit and gifts, God is also warning us that He will hold us responsible for what He has given us. In the Bible, God's Word, He reminds us "...to whom much is given, from him much will be required..." (Luke 12:48). That should be a sobering thought for every true believer. I do not want to be one of those who takes the prosperity of the Lord and spends it on my own desires.

That was exactly what was happening in the time of Joel. As a result, the very channel for Israel's prosperity—the crops—were cut off and the people came under judgment. Their land was overrun and ravaged by waves of insects. They represented the hordes of invading armies who would soon invade the land and plunder it. Yet, Joel informs the people that if they repent and turn back to the Lord these dreadful things will not happen. But he also prophesied that, despite his warnings, he knew the people were not going to take heed and save themselves from the judgment to come.

Joel was right. By the time a new generation came, the people did not remember the locust invasion or the prophecy of Joel. So once again, the nation of Israel suffered invasion and destruction from without. God's people would be attacked by the armies of the Assyrians—but destroyed by a lack of knowledge.

Believers Are the Life of a Nation

> "He has laid my vine waste and ruined my fig tree; he has stripped it bare and thrown it away; its branches are made white."

The fig tree is a type of the entire nation of Israel. The bark of the tree, like the vine, represents the believers within the nation—those who compose its protective and life-giving covering. When a nation's spiritual leaders fall, the nation is left wide open to destruction. When the bark is damaged enough, or in this instance, gone, the tree dies. God sees Israel as not only stripped of its bark but also white.

In the natural, there is no way for this nation of Israel to come back. But we serve the God of miracles. He still promises that believers in a nation can cause a seemingly dead tree to return to life. We form the life-giving fertilizer that can resurrect a seemingly dead tree back to life (Luke 13:6-9).

As the vine connected to grapes, the believers of a nation channel life from the Lord to the nation. They provide the sustenance of God's Word and the power of the Holy Spirit. God's life through us produces the true fruit in a nation.

Today we discuss our economic indicators, the gross national product, prime interest rate, wholesale price index, and more. We believe these things give us an indication as to where the nation is at the moment and where it is headed.

But as valid as all these things may be, the truth is that the real key factors in determining a nation's well-being are not economic but *spiritual*. The true "fruit bearers" in any nation are not its politicians, social reformers, industrialists, or entrepreneurs, but rather its faithful believers. A nation can boast the finest political, social, and economic leadership in the world, but if the believing remnant within the nation is not faithful to the ways and truth of the Lord, that nation can be destroyed.

The good news is that the exact opposite is also true. A nation can be filled with decadence in its leadership. But if the believers, the salt of the earth within it, remain faithful to their God, He can bless the land for their sakes. Remember, God does not spare any nation because of the *righteous, even a few, My people, who are called by My name. I sought for a man among them to stand in the gap.* This should be a source of great comfort and security to every believer in this land or any land! Make it your duty to pray for the country and give the gospel to the lost even if no one else is.

It is obvious the United States has long been blessed by God. But not because of the righteousness of its leaders, but because of the righteousness of His people within the borders. In view of our past sins and failures as a nation, by all rights, America should have been overthrown generations ago. But thank God for the remnant with this country who have held on to the promises of the Lord and prayed for our national leadership and all those in authority over us. Because of such people, our great nation has been protected and spared repeatedly.

And, although I do not see the righteousness I would like to see in our nation, I do see a rising number of believers returning to the Lord and His Word. There is a great hope on the horizon for our country or any country whose righteous ones continue to stand firm to pray, preach the gospel, teach the Word, raise up churches, and stand in faith each day on God's promises.

Stripped and looking worse than dead, Israel survived because God raised it from the dead. God raised His own Son from the grave and Jesus was not only physically dead but spiritually separated from God His Father while in the grave. Because God could raise Jesus from the dead and give Him eternal life, He can raise an individual from being spiritually dead and give them eternal life. A nation would be no different.

Israel was stripped of all life and God raised it up more than once. He will do it again when Jesus comes to reign eternally in His kingdom. That was the hope of the Israel of old, and that is the hope of any nation today, including the United States. For as bad as our situation may appear, God is still on His throne. And what is dead, God can raise to new life!

What are you facing? Does it look impossible? God thrives in our impossible situations. Turn your life over to Jesus if you have not received His salvation. Turn your spiritual life around. You have received salvation, ask for His forgiveness for your uncaring attitude toward God and His promises. He will pardon quickly and begin the process of bringing life back into your situation.

Israel's Lament

> 1:8 "Lament like a virgin girded with sackcloth for the husband of her youth."

Israel lamented in Joel's day after seeing the locust invasion that occurred. In this verse, Joel tells them, just as they are now weeping and mourning, so there is another day coming when they will cry and scream louder—when the waves of Assyrian troops come sweeping across Israel in the next generation. He compares the coming anguish to a young, newlywed bride who is weeping and mourning the death of her husband before their married life has even begun. She is called a virgin because she has not had a honeymoon yet; she has not had a night with him to make love and consummate the marriage.

This picture gave the children of Israel some idea of the tragic fate headed toward them. But Joel is telling them they still have time to turn the invasion around.

The Meal Offering

> 1:9 "The grain offering and the drink offering have been cut off from the house of the Lord; the priests mourn, who minister to the Lord."

The grain offering was the firstfruits of the crops with which the Lord had blessed the people. It is part of the offering of the Feast of Firstfruits. The offering of firstfruits was to be presented to the Lord at a specified time and dedicated to Him in recognition of His blessings on them.

Because of the destruction visited on the land by the locusts, there is no more grain to be offered before the Lord. But that really didn't matter. This offering became only a ritual—only an outward showing of something that took place long before. There had been no true offerings in the house of the Lord for many years because of the spiritual carnality of the people. It is not the ritual that counts with God, but the meaning and attitude behind the ritual. Now they were simply reaping the results of their years of indifference and disobedience to the Lord's command to bring the firstfruits of their crops into His house. It was no longer a means of worship to God accompanied by a corresponding life of holiness before Him.

This should be a lesson for us today as well. We should remember that whenever the Lord blesses His people, He expects to receive back the firstfruits of that blessing. God does not prosper His people just so they can hoard the prosperity—either to sit and watch it grow or to spend it on their own lusts. God intends His people to quickly return to Him the firstfruits, the tithe, of the abundance He has given them. This reinvestment of the Lord's blessings helps insure that God's covenant will be established on earth and His blessings will continue to return to us.

However, if God's people refuse to give back to the Lord the portion He has blessed them with, they open a door for the destroyer to come in and steal what God has given them. This had already happened once in Joel's day in the form of the invasion of the locusts. Now the prophet is warning Israel that it will happen again with the Assyrian invasion.

What was the meal offering exactly, which the Jews were supposed to be offering to the Lord? It is described in detail in the first 16 verses of Leviticus chapter 2. The first verse of that chapter summarizes it: "When anyone offers a grain offering to the Lord, his offering shall be of fine flour. And he shall pour oil on it and put frankincense on it."

There are three important things about this offering. First, it is a bloodless offering. This is not the offering of the atonement, the sacrificial lamb. This offering is a type of propitiation—an offering of satisfaction to the Lord. Propitiation simply means satisfaction. His satisfaction of His work. The issue is not that we are satisfied, but that God is eternally satisfied with the work of Jesus in death, burial, and resurrection for our sins.

The offering calls for fine flour, flour that has been ground to a powder-fine consistency. This speaks of how the body of our Lord was beaten and crushed for us, and of the three days and nights He spent in the heart of the earth (Psalm 22:14).

Next, oil was placed on the flour. In Romans 8:11 the apostle Paul tells us that the same Holy Spirit who raised Christ from the dead will one day make alive our mortal bodies. The oil was added as a type of the power of the Holy Spirit that came upon the Lord Jesus to resurrect Him from the grave.

Finally, frankincense was added to the flour. This speaks of the work of Jesus as He arose into heaven to take His place at the right hand of the Father. At that moment, Jesus' part in the work of salvation was complete. God the Father said to Him, "...Sit at My right hand, until I make your enemies your footstool" (Psalm 110:1). By giving Himself for us as an offering and a sacrifice to God, Jesus became a sweet-smelling aroma, a divine satisfaction, a propitiation to the Father (Ephesians 5:2).

Frankincense is a type of the aroma that filled the nostrils of God as Jesus completed His work of redemption and then sat down at the right hand of the Father in heaven. God had never been eternally satisfied with any offering of men or priests. He was only temporarily satisfied, appeased, and therefore needed more sacrifices. Jesus rose from the dead, ascended into heaven, and God the Father knew and proclaimed that no other sacrifice needed to be offered. God was eternally satisfied—propitiated—with the work of Jesus.

In Joel's day, the coming redemptive work of the Lord was not being taught by the priests to the people through their teaching or symbolically by their offerings. Knowledge and understanding of the remission of sins was gone. Through years of apathy on their part and negligence on the part of their spiritual leaders, the people of Israel lost touch with their heritage, and thus with their future.

The Drink Offering

Our verse says the meal offering and the *drink offering* are cut off from the house of the Lord. The drink offering was the wine poured over the offerings. Where the meal offering represented the broken body of Jesus, the wine was a type of the blood of the Lord Jesus Christ.

The next thing not being taught by the priests was the work of the blood of Jesus—the remission of sins. The people of Joel's day no longer had any understanding of Messiah's sacrifice, the shedding of His blood to remove and cleanse their sins. This knowledge also had been cut off from the people.

With that comprehension cut off from God's people, they had no place to go but downhill. Not being taught of the coming redemptive work of Jesus on the Cross, the people were left to their own devices for salvation and righteous living. Self-effort eventually wears out, and sublimation is substituted for faith—using a crutch of drinking and daily pleasures.

Symptoms of Apostasy

> 1:10 "The field is wasted, the land mourns; for the grain is ruined, the new wine is dried up, the oil fails."

Three things are mentioned in this verse: grain, wine, and oil. All three are normally used in the presentation of offerings to the Lord. They had been consumed by the famine brought on by the locust invasion. But it really didn't matter, because it had been years since all three had been used at all in temple worship. The priests had failed to make use of them to teach the people about the work of Jesus, their coming Messiah and Redeemer.

> 1:11 "Be ashamed, you farmers, wail, you vinedressers, for the wheat and the barley; because the harvest of the field has perished."

The vinedressers are those who tended the wine for the drink offerings. The farmers took care of the grain in the field, and the vinedressers tended the grapes on the vine.

Their titles have a deeper spiritual significance than their literal meaning. The spiritual leaders of the nation were the true farmers and vinedressers. They were the ones charged with the responsibility of teaching and instruction for the people of the nation of Israel. In other words, the oversight of the people's spiritual maturity was given to them by God. God's grain and grapes were the believers of Israel.

Jesus taught this in Matthew 21:33-46. He gave a parable to the religious leaders of Israel in His day. He told of a field that was turned over to farmers and vinedressers to care for it. But they failed to properly maintain the field. Because of their failure, Jesus said the field would be taken from them and turned over to others—a new group of faithful stewards. The religious leaders became angry after they heard the parable when they realized Jesus was speaking about them.

Jesus said because they had not been faithful, God was going to take His field from them and turn it over to another nation. That nation was the coming Church taken from all nations on earth. This event occurred on the day of Pentecost when the field was taken from the hands of the Jewish leaders and placed into the hands of the Church of Jesus Christ.

Today, we as Christians, are the farmers and the vinedressers of the Lord's field. The Lord of the harvest is saying to us, "Behold the fields are white unto harvest." As God's leaders, the farmers and vinedressers—the shepherds, the pastors, and teachers, we need to be teaching the truth of the Word of God to God's people who are winning souls each day, because "the harvest of the field is perishing."

> 1:12 "The vine has dried up, and the fig tree has withered; the pomegranate tree, the palm tree also, and the apple tree—all the trees of the field are withered. Surely joy has withered away from the sons of men."

The fig is dying because the vine has dried up. Believers are the vine, and the tree was Israel. Today, it is individual nations. "As goes the vine, so goes the tree." Don't place all blame on the leaders of our nation, a certain political group, party, or individual. As Christians, *you and I* are the major reason our nation spiritually prospers or declines.

Remember 2 Chronicles 7:14, "If *My people* who are called by *My* name will humble *themselves,* and pray and seek *My* face, and turn from *their* wicked ways, then I will hear from heaven, and will forgive *their* sin and heal *their* land." God must forgive *us* of *our* sins before He will heal the land. Contrary to what we have been led to believe for decades, this verse is not directed (nor does it refer to) the general population—it applies only to believers. Therefore, it is not the "sins of the nation" that God is concerned with here—it is the sins of His own people within the nation.

If we as Christians will repent and turn to God, He can heal our land despite bad leadership or legislation. He will heal it for *our* sake. And this verse is not demanding that all Christians within the nations repent. This would never happen. God is looking for a group who will stand and repent for their part in the hindering of God's blessing from being poured out. Small groups of dedicated believers, even individuals, are responsible in history for revivals in churches, cities, and nations. *"I sought for a man among them..."* (Ezekiel 22:30).

If you are salt, then act like it. Turn from your own selfishness and sinfulness and seek God's face for revival. Next, begin to witness to the world of God's grace to save. This is the Great Commission, and it has not changed. Responsibility does not begin with others—it starts with you. As good as a nation is, it is only temporary. But every soul you win and every disciple you raise up is eternal and brings praises before the angels around the throne of God in heaven.

Joel then speaks of the palm tree, a symbol of *praise*. Palm branches were used at the triumphal entry of Jesus into Jerusalem. "...when they heard that Jesus was coming to Jerusalem, took branches of palm trees and went out to meet Him, and cried out: 'Hosanna! Blessed is He who comes in the name of the Lord!...'" (John 12:12-13).

Because there was no more face-to-face communion with God, no more understanding of the blood sacrifice, and no more teaching of the significance of the grain offerings, there was no more *praise*. The *joy* in Israel was gone.

Finally, Joel speaks of the apple tree. In Song of Solomon 2:5, the Shulamite woman speaks to her shepherd lover: "...refresh [comfort] me with apples, for I am lovesick." This young woman was so lovesick for her lover that she was ready to faint, "comfort me *with apples*." In the ancient world, apples were used to restore consciousness. When the person fainted, an apple was quickly cut in two, and the pieces were passed beneath their nose, similar to smelling salts. The apple tree teaches how people can restore a broken fellowship with the Lord.

This restoration of fellowship is done with the "apple" of God's Word—specifically 1 John 1:9, "If we confess our sins, He is faithful and just to forgive us our sins and to cleanse us from all unrighteousness." Thank God for the "apple" of repentance and restoration.

In many ways, the most crucial thing that was not being taught to the nation of Israel was the simplicity of coming back to the Lord. The spiritual leaders were no longer teaching the people about confession and forgiveness of sins.

Does that mean that the concept and application of 1 John 1:9 is found in the Old Testament? Yes, it does. Remember how David had been out of fellowship with the Lord for a full year because of his sin with Bathsheba and the murder of her husband? Finally, when it became evident that David was not coming to Him, God sent the prophet Nathan to speak to the king.

What was the first thing David said when confronted with his guilt? "...I have sinned against the Lord..." (2 Samuel 12:13). Immediately Nathan said to him, "...The Lord also has put away your sin; you shall not die." A year's worth of sin was wiped out with one confession: "...I have sinned against the Lord...." What happened to cause such a transformation? By repenting of his sin, David took a sniff of the apple of restored fellowship and was instantly restored to favor with God.

Simply put, what was failing to be taught in the nation of Israel was first, worship; second, praise; and third, repentance. "Even *all* the trees of the field are withered." None of the aspects of the Word of God—righteousness, fellowship with the Lord, daily study of the Word, and the victorious life—were being taught. Everyone depended on financial blessings for their salvation and deliverance. In other words, they used the Word just long enough to become financially blessed. Then they dropped their trust in God and put their trust in money. What a sad state.

"All of the trees of the field are withered because joy is withered away from the sons of men." Because joy withers inside us. What happens inside a person directly affects what happens on the outside and is evident to all. The symptoms of apostasy become easy to perceive and recognize—dryness of spirit, loss of appetite for the Word of God, weakness of heart, and lack of the joy of the Lord. But what *can* be done about these things?

> 1:13 "Gird yourselves and lament, you priests; wail you who minister before the altar; come, lie all night in sackcloth, you who minister to my God; for the grain offering and the drink offering are withheld from the house of your God."

This is the remedy for apostasy: "Gird [Prepare] yourselves for coming trouble and lament, you priests." Joel lays the blame for the situation exactly where it belongs. Repentance must begin in the house of God.

> 1:14 "Consecrate a fast, call a sacred assembly; gather the elders and all the inhabitants of the land into the house of the Lord your God, and cry out to the Lord."

After the priests have sanctified themselves, they are to call in the congregation—the believers, the vine of the nation, the bark of the tree. They are to call that group of people to rededicate themselves to the Lord. Because when the bark is good, the tree will be good. A nation is blessed when believers are serving God. Even the citizens prosper when God's people become effective salt. Spiritual believers not only sanctify their place of worship, but also sanctify their homes and place of work.

Wherever effective Christians go, peace, harmony, and joy follows them and affects the world. This is not bragging on us as believers but bragging on Jesus in us. Joel is saying that God can turn a nation around if believers, the salt of the earth, will regain their savor.

3

THE RAPTURE AND SECOND COMING OF THE LORD

JOEL 1:15-20

THE DAY OF THE LORD

1:15 "Alas for the day! For the day of the Lord is at hand; it shall come as destruction from the Almighty."

1:16 "Is not the food cut off before our eyes, joy and gladness from the house of our God?"

1:17 "The seed shrivels under the clods, storehouses are in shambles; barns are broken down, for the grain has withered."

1:18 "How the animals groan! The herds of cattle are restless, because they have no pasture; even the flocks of sheep suffer punishment."

> *1:19 "O Lord, to You I cry out; for fire has devoured the open pastures, and a flame has burned all the trees of the field."*

> *1:20 "The beasts of the field also cry out to You, for the water brooks are dried up, and fire has devoured the open pastures."*

The Meaning of the Day of the Lord

The term *"the day of the Lord"* is a reference to end times. From the fall of man, God has stepped in at times to reconstruct what man has destroyed: the sacrifices, the flood to remove evil and begin again, the Tower of Babel, the ten plagues, and the parting of the Red Sea to deliver Israel are only a few of the times God has had to step in and correct what man and Satan have done.

But since Jesus' ascension and through the Church Age, God has been seated, and Jesus is also seated at the Father's right hand. "The Lord [Father] has said to my Lord [Jesus], "Sit at My right hand, till I make Your enemies Your footstool'" (Psalm 110:1). Throughout the 2,000 years of our dispensation, Jesus has had to set a number of things right; but as a whole, has left the Church in charge, having been given Jesus' authority against Satan and demons, and supernatural power to lay hands on the sick, and see them recover, and raise the dead. When Satan runs into a wise Christian, it is like meeting Jesus face-to-face all over again.

But as powerful as the Church is, we cannot correct the problems of the world's empires, and we were never told to do it. We are to win souls, get people filled with the Holy Spirit and God's Word, and make disciples out of each new believer. Only God, Jesus Himself, the Holy Spirit, and elect angels can bring the world out of the situation we see present now. Once Jesus comes for His Church and takes it into heaven, the Father and the hosts of heaven will go to work like never seen before to stop Satan, his demons, fallen angels, and man's armies during the Tribulation.

At the end of the seven years of Tribulation, it will look like Satan is going to win, but Jesus will return and destroy all the armies of the earth with the most powerful weapon in the universe—His voice. During these seven years, believers on earth will not be in bunkers or caves hiding from Satan and the devastation he is causing. They will be doing what every believer's job has been since the Old and New Testament began—winning souls and making disciples out of them. The Tribulation will be a time of the greatest evangelism the world has ever seen. People will be swept into the kingdom of God like never before because, where sin abounds, grace does much more abound (Romans 5:20). Sin will abound at record levels during the Tribulation. Believers will win souls and God will defeat Satan.

In our opening verse, "the day of the Lord" refers to the whole of the Tribulation, including the end, the return of the Lord Jesus to the earth to establish His kingdom. The Tribulation will begin immediately after the Rapture, the appearing of Jesus for His Church.

The Rapture of the Church Is an Ending and a Beginning

I must clear up the meaning of the word *rapture.* Although the word is often called the coming of the Lord, it is not a coming. The Rapture—the taking away of the Church—is an "appearing." Jesus never comes back to earth at the Rapture. He appears in the sky with the Church Age saints from heaven. They receive a resurrection body along with us; then Jesus gathers all members of the Church Age and takes them back to heaven to prepare them as His bride.

This will occur immediately after the Church has gone through the Judgment Seat of Christ and received rewards for their works on earth. This is not a judgment to see if members of the Church get to remain in heaven; this was a settled fact at their salvation. The Judgment Seat of Christ will see the burning up of our works done in the flesh (wood, hay, and straw) and a rewarding of our deeds done in the power of the Holy Spirit (gold, silver, and precious stones) (1 Corinthians 3:10-15). Jesus' second coming, the advent, will occur seven years later, after the Tribulation is over.

The Tribulation will be the completion of Daniel's 70 weeks (70 segments of 7 years, 490 years). At 483 years, Jesus went to the Cross and Daniel's 70 weeks were stopped. There is still seven more years of Jewish time to be fulfilled; the Tribulation. Another name for the Tribulation is Daniel's 70th week. The Tribulation will last for seven years, completing Jewish time, and will end at Jesus' second coming to end the Tribulation and begin the Millennium. This will be the beginning of the Millennium, the first 1,000 years of Jesus' eternal reign on earth.

After the Millennium, the earth will be renovated, and heaven will come and rest over Jerusalem. All sinners and the hosts of hell will be sent to the lake of fire and no sinners will exist on earth ever again. Then Jesus will rule from Jerusalem for eternity.

It has been told that Joel spoke prophetically of two coming invasions in the life of the nation of Israel. We learned that one these two events was the invasion of Israel by Assyria. In the day Joel wrote, the Assyrian invasion had not yet taken place. Yet we know with certainty that this prophecy was literally fulfilled.

All of God's Promises Are as Good as Done

This is the basis of our faith—what God has spoken, He will perform. Ezekiel 12:25 tells us, "For I am the Lord. I speak, and the word which I speak will come to pass...." This is why a knowledge of the Word of God is essential to faith. Our faith is not based on the words of men, but on the Creator of all things. He knows the future and what events will occur. He has let us know many events yet future in His Word. Without knowledge of the Word, we have no foundation for our faith. We know that as surely as God has told us what *has* happened, He has also told us what *will* happen.

In the first chapter of Joel, two future events are prophesied. Taking as his theme the locust invasion that had already occurred in his day, Joel spoke of two occurrences he said would take place in the existence of Israel. The first event already came to pass; the invasion of Israel by Assyria. This is now past history.

But Joel spoke just as assuredly of the coming of "the day of the Lord." As surely as Joel's prophecy of "the day of the Lord" was given, it will also be fulfilled. God sees the future as clearly as He sees today and the past.

Many of the things in the Word of God were prophecies in the day in which they were written. For example, the prophet Isaiah foretold the first coming of the Christ as a child to be born to a virgin (Isaiah 9:6). In chapter 53, Isaiah prophesied of Messiah's crucifixion and death, and of His bearing of our sins and sickness. At the end of chapter 53 into the beginning of chapter 54, Isaiah foretold of Christ's resurrection and spoiling of the kingdom of Satan. In Isaiah 28, the Day of Pentecost is prophesied—how "with stammering lips and another tongue" God would speak to His people.

Isaiah is only one author of many in the Old Testament who prophesied to Israel in their day of events yet to come. Other events such as the Tribulation, Jesus' second coming to the earth to reign, and the eternal kingdom were also foretold. With us, this is prophecy; with God, it is just fact. When we treat God's Word as fact, great things are about to happen. This is faith. Without faith, we cannot please God (Hebrews 11:6).

It stands to reason that if one part of the Word of God is true, the rest of it must also be true. If God fulfilled the words of His servants concerning the first coming of our Lord, it seems reasonable to believe that He will fulfill their words regarding His second coming. Based on what was written and has taken place in the history of Israel, it is certain the promised "day of the Lord" will come to pass just as it is prophesied.

The Coming of Jesus for the Church

> Now, brethren, concerning the coming of our Lord Jesus Christ and our gathering together to Him, we ask you, not to be soon shaken in mind or troubled, either by spirit or by word or by letter, as if from us, as though ***the day of Christ*** had come. Let no one deceive you by any means; for that Day will not come unless the falling away comes first, and the man of sin is revealed, the son of perdition, who opposes and exalts himself above all that is called God or that is worshiped, so that he sits as God in the temple of God, showing himself that he is God.
>
> Do you not remember that when I was still with you I told you these things? And now you know what is restraining, that he may be revealed in his own time. For the mystery of lawlessness is already at work; only He who now restrains will do so until He is taken out of the way. And then the lawless one will be revealed, whom the Lord will consume with the breath of His mouth and destroy with the brightness of His coming (2 Thessalonians 2:1-8).

"The day of Christ" in verse 2 is the same as "the day of the Lord" in Joel chapter 1. It refers to the same event—the return of the Lord Jesus Christ to this earth. Jesus' return is first to remove the Church, and seven years later to defeat the armies of the nations who attack Israel, then to rule the earth forever. Jesus Christ *is* the Lord of whom Joel spoke in the Old Testament.

In this passage in 2 Thessalonians 2:1-8, there is a coming mentioned in verse 1 and a coming in verse 8. These two comings are not the same event. The length of time of Satan's control over the earth, the Tribulation, will be seven years. It begins with a "coming"—Jesus for the Church—and ends with a "coming" of Jesus to judge, then rule over the earth.

The first coming of Jesus is in a split second when we, the Church, will receive a resurrection body and be taken to heaven with Jesus. The world will not see or hear His voice as He comes with a shout (1 Thessalonians 4:16). He will unite the living members of the Church on earth with those of the Church who have died and gone to heaven—the dead in Christ. He will purify the entire Church at the Judgment Seat of Christ, ridding us from all the works of the flesh—spots and wrinkles, wood, hay, and straw (1 Corinthians 3:10-15). We will then be prepared to return to earth with Jesus as His bride. This is the second mention of a "coming" of Jesus Christ in 2 Thessalonians 2:8.

So often we, as Christians, speak of looking forward to "the coming of the Lord." What we really mean to say is we are looking forward to the day when Jesus will return for us, "our gathering together unto Him." Then Jesus will "return to earth" seven years later as its eternal King and ruler. He will come "for" us, and then "with" us.

When Jesus comes for us to take us to heaven, it will occur in the clouds, "in the air" (1 Thessalonians 4:17), and it will be quickly, "in a moment, in the twinkling of an eye" (1 Corinthians 15:52). The word *moment* is the Greek word *atamo*, meaning a time period so small it cannot be further divided, indivisible. In one split second we will be here and then be gone. All of this occurs to take the family on earth to meet and be with the family in heaven. This event—the taking away, the Rapture of the Church—will occur seven years before the Lord Jesus returns to set foot on the earth to eternally rule all nations. On that day His feet will touch the Mount of Olives.

At the Rapture, the appearing of Jesus to take His Church to heaven, we are told "the dead in Christ will rise first" (1 Thessalonians 4:16). This is a reference to all who received Jesus during their lifetime, then died, left their body behind and went to heaven in spirit form. They will receive an eternal resurrection body first, then "we who are alive and remain shall be caught up together with them" (1 Thessalonians 4:17). We will receive a resurrection body as our present body is transformed into an eternal body. Then all—the dead in Christ and those who are alive and remain—will go to heaven with Jesus. It will happen so quickly the world will only know. All they can say is *we were here a split second ago, and now we are gone*. Jesus' next coming will be seven years later at the end of the Tribulation. We will return with Him in our resurrection bodies, as His bride. He will remain on earth to rule the kingdoms and nations of the world.

THE SEVEN YEARS OF TRIBULATION

The length of the Tribulation is seven years. It is divided into two periods of three and a half years. The first half is called the Tribulation. It will begin as a time of peace. The antichrist will present himself as a world leader of peace. Even though great problems are present in the world, he announces to the world that he has come to solve the world's problems and bring stability.

The second half is called the Great Tribulation. At this halfway point, the antichrist reveals himself as the son of Satan instead of the Son of God. He moves his rulership to Israel and into the temple, sitting on the throne reserved for the Messiah, Jesus Christ. He then begins an all-out attack on the Jewish people worldwide, to kill them. His plan is to destroy the Jewish nation and all Jews. If this is successful, Jesus will have no reason to rule from Jerusalem. God will have been proven to be a liar.

But God has a place of preservation prepared for the Jewish people—three mountain ranges (Matthew 24:15-16), foretold in the Old Testament as Edom, Moab, and Ammon (Daniel 11:41). If they remain there and do not leave, they will be spared by God's power to again occupy Israel and Jerusalem at the end of the Tribulation.

The Great Tribulation will be the worst time in all of earth's history (Matthew 24:21-22). At the end of the second half, Jesus will return to earth to remain forever as its King. He will remove the antichrist, the false prophet, the beast, the fallen angels released during the Tribulation, all demons, and finally all unbelievers from the earth. Then the earth and all creation will be released from the curse inflicted by Adam's transgression. It is recorded that even the mountains and hills will sing, and the trees will clap their hands (Isaiah 55:12).

The Coming of Jesus for the World

The Word of God is given to us to comfort and bring us hope for the days to come, just as it was for Joel's day. Just the mention of "end times" causes many to go into a panic. They see controlling government, wars, famines, starvation, and world panic on the horizon.

But Jesus told us of the signs of the end: "When you see these things begin to come to pass, then look up, and lift up your heads; for your redemption draweth nigh" (Luke 21:28 KJV). Instead of looking for the worst, look at end-time events and rejoice, even as they are presently beginning. Your Redeemer is coming soon.

Even those on earth during the rule of the antichrist are reminded of scripture: Jesus will destroy this wicked world ruler with the breath of His mouth and the brightness of His coming. Nothing Satan can create is bigger than Jesus and His power.

Jesus' coming for the world is seven years after His coming for the Church, with the Tribulation in between. But as surely as Jesus came for His Church, He will come for the nations of the world. So if you are concerned about the future, stop and remember the past. Has God always come through for you? *Yes!* Then He will come through again. He remains the same yesterday, today, and forever.

I am reminded of God's power when Israel was held captive by Egypt. Ten plagues came on Egypt, and yet after each one Pharaoh stood up to God. As Pharaoh rose up, so did God. When God sent a plague, Pharaoh rose up again to defy Him. God continued to send plagues, and Pharaoh continued to resist. Finally, Pharaoh rose as high as he could go, and God continued to rise higher. There is no height the world can rise to that God is not greater.

Even Satan and all the armies of the world cannot stand against Jesus from heaven. Jesus will return as lightning, with the redeemed Church—His bride—behind Him. He will open

His mouth, and a sharp two-edged sword will come out and slay all the armies of the world attacking Jerusalem and Jesus. One Man, God's Man, Jesus, will defeat all the armies of the world with God's Word coming from His mouth (Revelation 19:14-16).

If you have given your life to Christ, why do you fear? God is on your side, and you are on His. Because God can deliver the entire world through Jesus, He can certainly deliver you out of anything. What is your problem compared to the parting of the Red Sea, causing the River Jordan to back up, feeding more than 20,000 people with five small loaves of bread and two fish, and ultimately winning the battle of Armageddon against the armies of every nation in the world? Because God is for you, who can be against you? Or we could say, who in hell can be against you?

The Power of the Church

The coming of Jesus to remove His Church is necessary. The seven years of Tribulation cannot begin until the Church, the body of Christ, is removed. We are what is hindering the antichrist from even being revealed. He is probably in the world now but cannot take his throne or begin his rule until we are removed. Let's return to our opening scriptures for this chapter:

> Now, brethren, concerning the coming of our Lord Jesus Christ and our gathering together to Him, we ask you, not to be soon shaken in mind or troubled, either by spirit or by word or by letter, as if from us, as though the day of Christ had come (2 Thessalonians 2:1-2).

False teachers had come to Thessalonica telling the congregation they had heard from the Holy Spirit that Jesus had already come and the members of the church had missed it. They also told the congregation that Paul knew this to be true and had written another letter saying Jesus had already come and gone, leaving the believers behind at Thessalonica. The congregation began to fear, and panic set in. Paul writes again, telling them it was not true and not to believe the false teachers.

> Let no one deceive you by any means; for that Day will not come unless the falling away comes first, and the man of sin is revealed, the son of perdition (2 Thessalonians 2:3).

The Greek word for *falling away* is *apostasia*, a derivative meaning simply "to depart." Although it can be transliterated apostasy, its true meaning is "a departure" or "separation" from something, good or bad. Paul is letting the Thessalonians know that Jesus could not have come yet because the antichrist has not yet appeared. Jesus has to come for His Church first before the antichrist can even be revealed. The Church is what is keeping Satan's world leader from even showing himself.

The Amplified Bible footnotes this word as possibly meaning the "departure of the Church" must occur before the antichrist can be revealed. Kenneth Wuest comes closest to the original Greek of any I have found. He translates this sentence: "That day shall not come until the aforementioned departure of the church occurs first." *Aforementioned* is a reference to the Rapture of the Church in 2 Thessalonians

2:1, "the coming of our Lord Jesus Christ and our gathering together to Him."

In other words, even the appearing of the antichrist cannot occur until the Church is taken away first, and then "that man of sin will be revealed, the son of perdition; who opposes and exalts himself above all that is called God or that is worshiped, so that he sits as God in the temple of God, showing himself that he is God" (2 Thessalonians 2:3-4).

How powerful the Church of Jesus Christ is! And how powerless is Satan! For he cannot even reveal his "man of sin" until we, the Church, have been taken out of his way. Then, when we are taken into heaven with the Lord, the events of the Tribulation will take place.

Second Thessalonians 2:6-8 tells us of the power of the Church in the day we are living:

> And now you know what is restraining, that he may be revealed in his own time. For the mystery of lawlessness is already at work; only He who now restrains will do so until He is taken out of the way. And then the lawless one will be revealed, whom the Lord will consume with the breath of His mouth and destroy with the brightness of His coming.

The one restraining Satan's power on earth is not the Holy Spirit alone, but also the ones the Holy Spirit lives in—the Church of Jesus Christ. Though at times the Church seems weak, it is still powerful enough to keep Satan from ushering in the end times and revealing his false messiah, the antichrist. Satan's kingdom will be destroyed by the breath—the words—of Jesus Christ when He returns. This is told in Revelation 19:19-20.

But the actual revelation of the antichrist to the entire world will not occur until the middle of the Tribulation. In the first three and a half years he presents himself as a man and ruler of peace, even making a seven-year treaty of peace with Israel, saying he will protect the Jews and their nation. At the midpoint, the antichrist breaks his covenant with Israel and announces to the world exactly who he is—Satan's world ruler. This is why the second half of the Tribulation is called the Great Tribulation. Jesus called it the worst time in all world history, even stating that if He waited one more day to return to earth, no one would be alive (Matthew 24:21-22).

A Quick Review

Let's review the differences between the coming of Jesus for His Church—the Rapture—and Jesus' second coming to rule the earth.

First, they are two separate events seven years apart. At the Rapture of the Church, Jesus comes *for* His saints. Seven years later, He returns *with* His saints.

Second, at the Rapture of the Church, only the redeemed will see and hear Him. According to Paul, only the Church will hear the trumpet of God, and only the Church will hear the shout of the Lord Jesus Christ. At the coming of Jesus at the end of the Tribulation, every eye will see Him and every tongue will confess He is Lord. I remember when I was a student in Bible school under Brother Charles Duncombe, who was a master teacher on the subject of end times, a student asked if there were any scriptures left to be fulfilled before Jesus returned for us. Brother Duncombe responded, "Yes—the shout." That is all that is left, and we should expect that shout every day.

Third, at the Rapture of the Church, the Lord will not actually set foot on the earth; He only appears in the sky. The Church rises to meet Him in the air. The unbelievers—the rest of the world—do not see Him, nor do they hear Him. All they know is that one second we were here and the next split second *(atamo)* we were gone. At Jesus' second coming, His feet will stand on the Mount of Olives; there will be an earthquake; the mountain will split in two, create a valley, and a river will come out of the mountain and run toward the Mediterranean Sea (Zechariah 14:4).

Fourth, at the Rapture of the Church, there will be no flash of light when Jesus comes to take His Church. But at His second coming to rule the earth, He will return with the Church as lightning from the east to the west (Matthew 24:27). When Jesus was on the mountain with Peter, James, and John, He gave them a preview of what He will look like at His return to rule the earth. His face shone like the sun, and His clothing was as white as light (Matthew 17:2). We will discuss the reason for the necessary light of Jesus to be so bright at the closing of the book in Joel chapter 3.

The Two Witnesses

Accompanying Jesus on the mountain were the spirits of two Old Testament heroes, Moses and Elijah (Matthew 17:3). The disciples saw and recognized them. I believe these are the two witnesses of Revelation 11:3-6 who come back to the earth during the second half of the Tribulation.

John wrote of these two, saying one has the power to shut up the heavens so no rain would fall. Elijah did this in his day, and it did not rain for three and a half years on earth—the length of the second half of the Tribulation. And the second witness has power over waters to turn them to blood and to strike the earth with all types of plagues. Moses did this in Egypt with the Nile River, turning it to blood, and then brought more plagues throughout the land of Egypt afterward.

The Kingdom Comes

The millennial reign of Jesus will begin with people in resurrected bodies who came from heaven with Jesus, plus those people on the earth who were born again during the Tribulation and stood on the Word of God "to the end." These are the people who will enter the millennial reign with Jesus. They will have long lives restored to them. Death will be removed from the earth. This is the time mentioned by Isaiah when a child will "die" at the age of 100 (Isaiah 65:20). This does not literally mean the child will die physically at 100 but will leave childhood behind and enter adulthood. Today we consider the beginning of adulthood to be about age 18 to 21. Can you imagine a time when adulthood will not even begin until age 100?

At this time, disease, death, and destruction will be removed from the earth, and all creatures will live together in peace and harmony. The Bible says the lion will lie down with the lamb and that "nations...shall beat their swords into plowshares, and their spears into pruning hooks; nation shall not lift up sword against nation, neither shall they learn war anymore" (Isaiah 2:4).

Until the Lord Jesus returns to earth to set up His kingdom, there will be wars and rumors of wars. In fact, the world's greatest war is yet to be fought. Until Jesus returns in glory, nation will continue to war against nation. Jesus said so. But He also promised peace to those who believe and trust in Him. As Christians, we can live in a world full of war and violence and yet have peace in our hearts and minds.

"For as lightning comes out of the east, and shines to the west, so also will the coming of the Son of Man be" (Matthew 24:27). Note carefully: this is not the Rapture of the Church. At the Rapture, Jesus will not come as lightning out of the east to the west. According to Paul, Jesus will appear in the sky, and we believers will rise to meet Him in the air and go with Him into heaven (1 Thessalonians 4:16-17). The world will not know anything has happened, except we were here—then suddenly gone.

But at the time of the second coming, Jesus will come back as lightning from the east to the west. Why will He come back as lightning? The answer is found in the next verse, Matthew 24:28 (NIV): "Wherever there is a carcass, there the vultures will gather." This is a reference to the ending of the battle of Armageddon. In that day, Israel will have about as much defense against her enemies as a dead carcass does against vultures. Like a dead carcass, Israel will be surrounded by vultures—enemies coming in to feed off a dead animal.

As all the nations are circling Israel to pounce on her, suddenly the sky will go black, and a supernatural darkness taught later in Joel will come to pass. The sun and moon will no longer be seen, and the stars will not appear, just as the enemies of Israel are about to launch their attack. This is the darkness we have already discussed, which will last for 24 hours, immobilizing the armies and the people who operate them. No one will be able to move.

But after 24 hours of darkness, the lightning will be blinding. Jesus and all the saints in heaven will come at the end of the 24 hours of darkness as lightning, and every eye will see Him, and every knee will bow to Jesus, and every tongue will confess that Jesus is Lord. But for many it will be too late.

Jude 14 quotes Enoch, telling another side of the same story: "Behold, the Lord comes with ten thousands of His saints." The earth will be lit by God's glory as Jesus returns in great power.

The first thing removed from earth will be physical death. Sinners will run everywhere, trying to escape the wrath of the Lord. They will ask the mountains to fall on them. They will try to commit suicide. But death will flee from them (Revelation 6:16). They will have to stand before the Lord Jesus, who will separate the sheep—those saved during the Tribulation—from the goats—those who rejected Jesus during the Tribulation (Matthew 25:31-33).

Gospel Witnessing During the Tribulation

Many millions will be saved during the Tribulation. Throughout the book of Revelation, four different means are taught by which people will have an opportunity to accept Jesus during the worst time in all the history of mankind.

First, there will be 144,000 witnesses who will be preaching the gospel during the first half of the Tribulation (Revelation 7:4-8). These are 12,000 out of each of the twelve tribes of Israel.

Second, the tribulation saints themselves will be witnessing. These are those who will be born again during the Tribulation and will go out to win others to the Lord (Revelation 14:12-13).

Third, angels will be preaching the gospel during the Tribulation (Revelation 14:6-7). Because of the intensity of the time, angels will be ministering the plan of salvation, which is quite unusual. This occurred only a few times in the Old Testament, and never during the New Testament. During the Tribulation it will be a common occurrence.

Fourth, there will be the two witnesses we spoke of—Moses and Elijah—preaching the gospel also during the second half of the Tribulation (Revelation 11:1-7).

Then, immediately after the Tribulation, the sun will become dark, and the moon and stars will not give their light (Matthew 24:29). Again, this is not speaking of the Rapture, but seven years afterward, at the end of the Tribulation, when Jesus returns to earth to reign. It goes on to tell that the nations will mourn. These are those within each nation who survived the Tribulation but never accepted Jesus. It is hard to imagine, with all the supernatural anger of Satan being poured out and the protection provided by God, that many would still say "no" to accepting Jesus. Yet it will happen.

JOEL'S THIRD PROPHECY

At the beginning of our study of Joel's book, we taught that the first chapter contained an outline of the entire book. This outline was broken down into three parts. Part one (verses 1-5) dealt with the invasion of the locusts. Part two (verses 6-14) taught of the Assyrian invasion of Israel in the generations following Joel's life and writings. Finally, part three (verses 15-20) prophesies of the second coming of the Lord Jesus Christ.

Notice the Rapture of the saints is not mentioned in the outline—and for good reason. The Rapture is not prophesied anywhere in the Old Testament.

You may say, "But the Old Testament is filled with references to the coming of Jesus!" Yes, that is correct—the second coming of the Lord, but not the Rapture of the saints. Don't try to read the Rapture into the Old Testament. The Old Testament saints did not know anything about the Rapture of the Church because they did not know what the Church was. The Church was a mystery to them—something unknown in the Old Testament but revealed in the New Testament.

It is certain that if they did not know about the Church, they did not know anything about the Rapture of it. The Old Testament foretells only the second coming of the Lord. This helps us understand the end of the first chapter of Joel.

> 1:15 "Alas for the day! For the day of the Lord is at hand; it shall come as destruction from the Almighty."

For many years ministers have taught that God cannot destroy—that it is against His divine nature to bring destruction. But the same God who brings destruction here is the same God who destroyed the civilizations in a flood when they all turned against Him and His righteousness. He is also the same God who destroyed their Tower of Babel. God is very much in the business of destruction when the world flaunts its godless creations in His face and when His patience comes to a point where He can no longer tolerate humanity's sins.

There is a day coming when God is going to remove the Church from the earth. The Tribulation is then going to be the day of vengeance of God against those who have rejected Him and who continue to reject Him throughout the Tribulation. But even during the pouring out of His wrath on the earth, God is still going to exercise grace and mercy on those who will turn from their sins and receive His Son, Jesus Christ. He is going to spare them by covering them with His hand, teaching them to endure through the terrible time of suffering and torment. That is what Jesus meant when He told His disciples in Matthew 24:13, "But he who endures to the end [of the Tribulation] will be saved." This verse does not refer to us. It is not teaching about our enduring through life so we can just "squeak" into heaven. Christianity is not an endurance contest. It is a wonderful life—eternal and abundant.

The people Jesus was referring to here are those who are going to be born again during the Tribulation. He is saying that if they will endure to the end by standing on the promises of God, He will see to it at His second coming that they will be spared and will be ushered into His millennial reign. But those who do not accept Jesus during the Tribulation are going to be removed from the earth. This is exactly the opposite of the Rapture. At the Rapture, believers are going to be caught away into heaven. At the second coming of the Lord, unbelievers are going to be caught away into hell. In hell there will be weeping and wailing and gnashing of teeth. The unbelievers will be cast into outer darkness.

The only people left on earth to begin the millennial reign will be believers. That is one reason why that period will be a time of universal peace—a 1,000-year honeymoon for Jesus and His bride. Yet during the Millennium—1,000 years of peace after Jesus comes back to reign—people will be born on earth who will reject Jesus. Even in a perfect environment, with no Satan and Jesus ruling the earth, people will reject Him. God solves this at the end of the Millennium.

Those who rejected Jesus during the thousand years will be destroyed and sent to be with the multitudes in hell, to then stand before the Great White Throne Judgment (Revelation 20:11-15). This will be the final judgment for all who rejected Jesus. From this judgment, all who are in hell will be sent to the lake of fire eternally, including all sinners, Satan, the antichrist, fallen angels, and demons. Then the newly purified earth will enter the eternity of eternities, filled only with saints in resurrection bodies, angels, the Holy Spirit, Jesus Christ, and God the Father.

BACK TO THE TRIBULATION

> 1:16 "Is not the food cut off before our eyes, joy and gladness from the house of our God?"

This is a prophecy of the Tribulation to the inhabitants of Joel's day. Why is the Tribulation going to occur? Because, just as in the days of the locust invasion and in the days of the Assyrian invasion, the spirituality of the nation of Israel will have diminished—the nation will have become religious rather than righteous.

Woe to any person or people who becomes religious rather than spiritual. There is a big difference. Today the nation of Israel is very religious. But it is not religion that will save us or carry us through the perilous times ahead. There is going to be a remnant in Israel who will arise, accept Jesus as their Savior, and live daily by God's Word. They will be the salt of the nation of Israel. Even in the time of Tribulation, Israel as a nation will be spared because of the salt of the earth who will emerge.

Notice the food is cut off as a result of the spiritual life of the nation being cut off. It is the spiritual life that provides the hedge of protection around a person or a people. Whenever that spiritual life is kept strong, physical catastrophe is minimized and sometimes averted. But when the spiritual defense of a nation becomes weak, calamity will befall.

> 1:17 "The seed shrivels under their clods; storehouses are in shambles; barns are broken down, for the grain has withered."

The storehouses or granaries were the bins in which grain was stored. At the time of the harvest, the ancient Jews would take the harvested grain and put it into the storehouse and throw away the chaff. This is taught in Matthew 3:12, when John the Baptist spoke about the coming of the Lord Jesus, saying Messiah would thoroughly purge His floor (the earth), putting the grain into the storehouse but throwing out the tares, or chaff, to be burned. The grain represents believers. As the grain went into the bin, so the believers will go into the millennial reign with the Lord Jesus. But the chaff, representing sinners, will be burned up with unquenchable fire. Thus Joel predicts that physical calamity is going to come upon the nation of Israel because of their diminishing spiritual life.

> 1:18 "How the animals groan! The herds of cattle are restless, because they have no pasture; even the flocks of sheep suffer punishment."

Why do the beasts groan? Because there is no food for them—no grass or grain to eat. The cattle wander around, perplexed, because they can find no pasture. The sheep suffer punishment and are made desolate. This means the sheep are mostly dead and the rest are dying. They are weaker than cattle and cannot last as long.

> 1:19-20 "O Lord, to You I cry out; for fire has devoured the open pastures, and a flame has burned all the trees of the field. The beasts of the field also cry out to You, for the water brooks are dried up, and fire has devoured the open pastures."

This passage from Joel's day clearly indicates that, in the last days, there is going to come out of the nation of Israel a remnant who will cry to the Lord. And God is going to respond to their cry.

Not everyone in Israel is going to reject the Lord, just as not everyone throughout the rest of the world is going to reject Him during the Tribulation. In fact, the Tribulation is going to be one of the greatest times of evangelism the world has ever seen. Most of the teaching we hear about this time period emphasizes the trials and tribulations—the wars and ills and suffering—of this terrible seven-year period.

Of course, there will be much suffering. But when was the last time you heard any teaching about the massive evangelism that will take place during the Tribulation—and about the huge numbers of people who will turn to the Lord during that time?

It is going to happen. In fact, the masses are going to be so great they are going to populate the earth during the beginning of the Millennium. They are the ones who are going to reproduce children and see a population explosion that will then occupy earth into the eternity of eternities after the Millennium.

The fire mentioned here in these two verses is not just a physical fire, but a holocaust brought upon Israel by her enemies. This fire represents the weapons of destruction trained on Israel by the invading armies who war against her in this massive battle yet to come.

Right now the whole world is arming to the teeth. This is not by accident, nor is it without significance. There is coming a day when the enemies of Israel are going to surround her and turn all their armaments against her in an effort to wipe Israel off the face of the earth. The book of Daniel lists some of the nations that are going to fall—including Egypt, Jordan, and others—and those that will escape—Edom, Moab, and Ammon—the nations that will not yield to the pressures of the antichrist and his armies.

But Israel will be the main target of all the military might of her enemies, who will send against her a tremendous and vicious army equipped with the latest destructive weapons. Outnumbered and out-armed, surrounded on all sides and faced with total annihilation, the remnant of the nation of Israel—the salt of that nation—will cry out to God to save them.

And at the last moment, just before the instant of complete and utter destruction, God will intervene by sending Jesus, their Messiah, accompanied by His saints and holy angels. This will be the second advent—the second coming of the Lord Jesus—to save God's chosen people and the nation, Israel.

4

THE LORD'S TRUMPET

JOEL 2:1-14

The first chapter of Joel included an outline of the entire book and a prophetic look into the future of Israel all the way to the coming of Jesus Christ to rule the world. This outline was given through four locust invasions that came to Israel, each one more destructive than the previous.

The final invasion so devastated Israel, it seemed as if the nation would never survive. The four locust invasions foretold: first, of two coming Assyrian attacks by two different kings; followed by a third future attack by Rome, which would scatter the nation of Israel into the other nations of the world. The fourth attack is yet to come from an international army headed up by the antichrist, named in the Bible as the battle of Armageddon.

The story of the four invasions and God's ability to protect Israel, despite the size and power of the enemy, told the people

God had a future for His people and that no weapon of any size would prosper against them.

Now, beginning with Joel chapter 2, we take a detailed look at Armageddon. The first 14 verses of chapter 2 present a view of the battle of Armageddon from inside the city of Jerusalem. Verses 15 to the end of the chapter move outside the city and tell of the return of Jesus to save Israel from the attacking armies of the world. Jesus will then take His eternal rulership of the world as He sits on the temple throne in Jerusalem. And finally, chapter 3 is a view of the attack of Jesus Himself from outside Jerusalem, in the enemy's camp.

With all this in mind, let's take a close look at the first 14 verses of the second chapter of Joel.

Sound the Alarm

> 2:1 "Blow the trumpet in Zion and sound an alarm in My holy mountain! Let all the inhabitants of the land tremble; for the day of the Lord is coming, for it is at hand."

"Blow the trumpet in Zion" is a call to battle. It is not a trumpet—this is not an instrument of music—but a ram's horn, a shofar. Later, in verse 15, Joel says, "Blow the trumpet in Zion, sanctify a fast, call a solemn assembly" (Joel 2:15 KJV). In that verse, a trumpet will be a true trumpet.

The shofar of verse 1 introduces an assembly of the troops to fight the battle of Armageddon. The trumpet in verse 15 sounds a call to assemble the elect from the four winds and join the millennial reign of Jesus.

"Sound an alarm in My holy mountain...for the day of the Lord is coming." The day of the Lord is the day of the second advent, or arrival, of Jesus when He will come from heaven with His saints and angels to bring an end to the battle of Armageddon and begin His 1,000-year reign on earth.

THE APPROACHING ARMY

Before Jesus leaves heaven to return to earth in glory, several events will take place first. As Joel chapter 2 opens, we find one of these events. Israel is surrounded by her enemies gathered on her borders, like vultures around a dead carcass. The ram's horn is blown to sound the alarm. The time of the invasion has arrived.

> 2:2 "A day of darkness and gloominess, a day of clouds and thick darkness, like the morning clouds spread over the mountains. A people come, great and strong, the like of whom has never been; nor will there ever be any such after them, even for many successive generations."

"A people come, great and strong." In this verse we see an army that covers the land like a plague of locusts coming against Israel. So many are on the land and in the air that the sun is blotted out by their numbers. Like clouds of swarming insects, they come, blanketing the sky and land like thick darkness.

In Joel's day, locust swarms were commonplace. They were so thick they blotted out the light of the sun at midday, and so noisy they could be heard coming for miles in every direction. So devastating, they struck terror in the hearts of the bravest of men. At the sight and sound of such hordes of devouring attackers, the people shook in fear because there was nothing they could do to stop it.

Joel is saying an attack of locusts is the best comparison to the attack against Jerusalem at Armageddon. This huge and numberless army will descend on the tiny nation of Israel. The people will see and hear them approaching like giant clouds of locusts, laying waste to everything in their path. Never before has such an army existed, and never again in human history will there be one like it.

"*Like the morning spread over the mountains.*" Isn't it beautiful to watch the sunrise over mountains? But before the sun makes its appearance over the mountaintops, its light shines through and around the mountains. The rising of the sun can be anticipated before it actually takes place. But what can be done to stop it? Nothing. No matter how mighty or courageous a person or people may be, there is no power on earth strong enough to hold back the dawn.

This is how it will be when this enormous army begins its final assault on Israel. Joel says Israel will look across the mountains outside of Jerusalem and see and hear the marching hordes. Though they can see and hear the armies coming, they will be powerless to prevent the attack on Jerusalem and their own deaths. The army will come pouring through the mountain passes and over the tops of the hills like waves of the ocean rolling in on the beach. As they flood everything in their path, they will be as unstoppable as the sunrise. Nothing will be able to hold them back.

"*The like of whom has never been, nor will there ever be any such after them, even for many successive generations.*" There will never be another earthly army like this one, and for a very good reason. From the view of the enemy, the battle is intended to wipe out Israel forever. From God's view, this battle will usher in the eternal reign of the Lord Jesus Christ.

I think many inhabitants of Jerusalem, on that day, will remember the prophecy of Joel. Jesus Christ will appear personally to defeat this huge army and deliver His people. I hope this thought crosses your mind too: no matter how big Satan's attack may be against you, no matter how powerful your situation looks, and how powerless you feel—*because God is for you, who can be against you?* The God who split the Red Sea to deliver His people and caused the earth to stop its rotation so Joshua could win a battle, is your God too. One Man, Jesus Christ, will win this battle and defeat the giant army coming against His people. He has never failed and will never fail. He is on your side, and you are on His.

> 2:3 "A fire devours before them, and behind them a flame burns; the land is like the Garden of Eden before them, and behind them a desolate wilderness; surely nothing shall escape them."

In front of the invading armies of the antichrist will be huge flames of fire caused by the enemy's flamethrowers. This creates great explosions and rapidly spreading fire, causing the fields to burn and giving no place for the military of Israel to hide. This is the cause of all the destruction we read about at the end of chapter 1.

"*The land is as the Garden of Eden before them, and behind them is a desolate wilderness.*" The land looked like a beautiful garden in front of the invading armies, but the military burned it all. By the time the armies marched through the field, the field was gone. Now all that was left was bare ground and small fires.

If you go to Israel today you will see the Jewish people have turned what used to be dry, barren land into lush fields of fruits and vegetables. Through creative ways to conserve water, combined with new methods to grow crops, Israel has turned the desert into a garden, an abundant land of crops and vegetation. Fulfilling Isaiah 35:1, the desert now blossoms like a rose. And it will continue to blossom as the rightful owners of the land remain. This is God's land for God's people.

But the incoming armies of nations who hate Israel will want to turn this beautiful garden into an ash heap. This is a description of what the land looked like after four invasions of locusts had come through. Joel likens this invading army to the hordes of locusts that blotted out the sun and completely stripped away the land and vegetation.

You can see why Joel described the four locust invasions as plagues, each one worse than the ones before. Perhaps Joel had a vision of this coming destruction and had a limited vocabulary to describe it. These are weapons we understand today, but Joel was looking thousands of years into the future. He did his best, but he had never seen military machines and means of destruction like the armies of the antichrist.

But no matter how good their weapons and machinery are, they cannot beat Jesus Himself, who will conquer them all in a matter of minutes. The God of Abraham, Isaac, Jacob—and Jesus—will defend Israel.

Is Jesus your Defender? He must first be your Savior. By accepting Him as the Lord of your life, you belong to God.

And once you belong to Him, He will defend you in the worst of situations.

The antichrist has a plan to take Jerusalem in two days. He successfully makes it through the first day with little to no resistance and plans to finish the job the next day. Even with only one day left, Jesus will stop all of the antichrist's goals and Satan's plans. And at the end of the battle, instead of the antichrist seated in the temple of God, Jesus will be there. Remember, if Jesus is your Lord, you can also claim Him as your Defender.

> 2:4 "Their appearance is like the appearance of horses; and like swift steeds, so they run."

This verse speaks of the precision of this army—an obvious reference to tanks and other armored vehicles. To the eyes of an ancient prophet like Joel, who was seeing all these events ahead of time in a vision, a modern, technologically equipped army must have been beyond his powers of description. The speed and maneuverability of self-propelled war machinery could only be likened, in Joel's day, to a troop of well-trained and well-armed cavalry operating in unity and precision like never seen before.

> 2:5 "With a noise like chariots over mountaintops they leap, like the noise of a flaming fire that devours the stubble, like a strong people set in battle array."

Joel is impressed with their precision, and he is also amazed by their agility to leap over mountains in full battle gear. I don't want to date this book, but this so reminds me of movies such as *Star Wars* where legions of droid armies march in perfect order and can jump from the ground to the tops of walls and then run atop the walls with great speed.

AI (artificial intelligence) will definitely increase and continue, and many fears will come to pass. Armies will one day be mostly mechanical and electrical, computer driven. But who knows? What Joel saw was probably far beyond what I can even imagine. But whatever the best and greatest man is able to create, God is still greater.

Joel tried to describe the battle and weapons used and simply said it was like the noise of a flaming fire that will strike terror in the hearts of those who see and hear it.

What Joel saw was simply the first waves of attack from this devouring army as the nation of Israel and the city of Jerusalem watch in amazement and horror. The stubble was not just the trees and vegetation, but the very inhabitants of Israel. What fear must grip the people as they try to keep their trust in God, whose deliverance is so close.

> 2:6 "Before them the people writhe in pain; all faces are drained of color."

"*The people writhe in much pain.*" Literally this expression means "to be in anguish." The anguish of what has been destroyed is mixed with the fear of what is about to happen. The Hebrew literally says their faces are white. They are not just drained of color but are as pale as possible because of fear and anguish.

> 2:7 "They run like mighty men, they climb the wall like men of war; everyone marches in formation, and they do not break ranks."

A number of years ago, a popular chorus was sung making us the ones who climb the walls and march in formation without breaking rank as the armies of God, declaring His Word. I must point out that, in light of this prophecy of Joel, that just does not make any sense.

The truth is, you and I are not going to be part of the army that will rush on the city and run on the walls of Jerusalem! This is a description, not of "the army that carries out God's Word," but of a demon-possessed army that will enter the city to carry out the will of Satan and destroy Jerusalem.

This passage is actually a distress call, an alarm to awaken the people of Israel, to warn them of the destruction that is about to fall on them at the hands of this ruthless and seemingly unbeatable enemy.

"And they do not break ranks." This will be one of the finest-tuned military organizations in history. Satan will have assembled the most disciplined force the world has ever seen.

> 2:8 "They do not push one another; everyone marches in his own column. Though they lunge between the weapons, they are not cut down."

"They do not push one another." This is really a poor translation. The Hebrew says, "one shall not crowd the other." This testifies to the discipline and training of the troops involved.

This will be a coordinated attack—a team effort of the highest order. Every man will hold his position. He will march straight ahead, not seeking individual victory or recognition, never crowding or jostling his fellow soldier on either side. This army will present a truly unified front as it marches forward, rank after rank.

"Though they lunge between the weapons, they are not cut down." This phrase could also be better translated; it should read, "When they break through the defenses, they shall not change their course."

In addition to firm discipline and coordinated effort, this army will have great advantage—unity of purpose. They will march forth as one man, with one common, demon-inspired objective: the total annihilation of the nation of Israel and God's chosen people, the Jews who live there.

> 2:9 "They run to and fro in the city, they run on the wall; they climb into the houses, they enter at the windows like a thief."

"They run to and fro in the city." Despite the best efforts of the defenders, this army will run through the city of Jerusalem at will, wreaking havoc as they go. Before such an army, there will be no hope of escape, no place of refuge. Nothing and no one will be safe from them. The city will be theirs for the taking.

> 2:10 "The earthquakes before them, the heavens tremble; the sun and moon grow dark, and the stars diminish their brightness."

Just when things are at their worst, something strange occurs. God sends a supernatural earthquake. The sun will not shine, and the moon will be darkened. The stars will not show light, and the earth will be dark for a day. For 24 hours the entire earth will be held captive under a paralyzing blanket of darkness.

During these 24 hours, God is going to give the world one last chance to accept Jesus as their Savior. The last chapter of

Joel deals with the great battle that will be fought in the Valley of Megiddo. Joel refers to it as the "valley of decision" (Joel 3:14).

For 24 hours the enemies of God will have one final opportunity to decide to accept Jesus Christ and be saved. At the end of that period of darkness—that long night of decision—it will be too late. For then, in a flash like lightning, the Lord Jesus will make a grand entrance to earth. At that point, every eye will see Him and every tongue will confess that Jesus is Lord. But for those who waited until the 24 hours were over, it will be too late.

The Lord's Army

> 2:11 "The Lord gives His voice before His army, for His camp is very great; for strong is the One who executes His word. For the day of the Lord is great and very terrible; who can endure it?"

"And the Lord gives His voice before His army." Who is going to be in the army of Jesus Christ? *You and me!* The army of the Lord Jesus is going to be made up of innumerable angels and "ten thousands" of the saints of God who have been in heaven with Him for the past seven years, preparing for this glorious return of Jesus and His bride to earth.

This army will come from heaven with the Lord Jesus to rescue God's people, Israel. But neither the angels nor God's people will fight. Jesus will personally fight this battle—one Man against the massive number of soldiers and the best-equipped army in the world. Jesus will win, and the entire army will be slain. What a glorious day of victory that will be!

The army of Satan will attempt to overpower the army of the Lord—that mighty army of which you and I will be a part. But we will not have to rush on the city or run on the wall. That won't be necessary. None of us will have to raise a finger; we will not even have weapons. Only Jesus will be armed.

He will speak, and from His mouth will come a sharp two-edged sword, the spoken Word of God. His Word will go forth to destroy the armies of Satan that have come against Israel (Revelation 19:15).

Revelation 14:20 says on that day the blood of the enemy will run to the height of the horses' bridles. With the destruction of their enemies by the Lord Jesus, Israel will be spared and humbled. They will be saved and delivered by the Man they crucified.

As Zechariah says, "...they will look on Me whom they pierced. Yes, they will mourn for Him as one mourns for his only son and grieve for Him as one grieves for a firstborn" (Zechariah 12:10).

> 2:12 "Now, therefore," says the Lord, "turn to Me with all your heart, with fasting, with weeping, and with mourning."

"*Now, therefore, turn to Me.*" The word *now* means that today is the day of salvation. Joel is exhorting his fellow Jews in his day to turn from their evil life and accept God's plan of salvation through Jehovah—Jesus.

Joel knew the day was coming and exhorted his friends, family, and citizens to accept the Lord before it was too late. He likely knew the day of the Lord would come long after the citizens of Jerusalem in his day would be dead.

Our call to those who need Jesus should be the same. We are to witness to those who don't know Jesus as their Savior to accept Him now. Because the Bible teaches, "It is appointed unto man once to die, and after this the judgment" (Hebrews 9:27). That tells us most people will die before the end-time appearance of Jesus comes. That is why today is the day of salvation. If you die today, then tomorrow will be too late.

"*Turn to Me with all your heart, with fasting, with weeping, and with mourning.*" The message of salvation should be received with humility and respect toward God, and true repentance in our own hearts. God wants a complete giving of ourselves to Him, without argument. Also, with weeping for our lack of concern about eternity, and mourning for our disregard of God, His plan, and His love for all people.

Fasting is mentioned also because we need to know salvation is the most important thing in life—even more than our air, and even more than our necessary food and water.

Joel is also teaching that a life given to Jesus should show change. Our priorities should change, as well as our lifestyle. Not everyone changes at the same pace, and we should not be so quick to criticize people because their habits have not changed as quickly as we think they should. It usually takes time for the new nature to bring maturity and replace carnality. It takes time for us to produce works that show repentance (Acts 26:20).

> 2:13 "So rend [tear] your heart, and not your garments; return to the Lord your God, for He is gracious

and merciful, slow to anger, and of great kindness; and He relents from doing harm."

This verse is telling the citizens of Nineveh to tear their hearts, not just their clothing. Don't make repentance only an outward act, but let the act reflect a true heart of remorse and pain for opposing God and His Word.

Repentance is not a façade but a face that shows outwardly what the hidden heart is experiencing. Many sinners claim to know the Lord and may have an outward appearance of morality and the appearance of true salvation. But these are the ones Jesus will expose when He tells them one day, "I tell you I do not know you, where you are from. Depart from Me, all you workers of iniquity" (Luke 13:27).

We look on the outward appearance, but God looks on and knows the heart. These verses in Joel are not speaking to sinners, but to believers who have accepted the Lord. Not only can sinners be hypocrites, but so can believers. The outward acts of righteousness must be an expression of true spirituality and cleanliness of heart.

It will not be those who have made an outward show of "tearing their garments" who will be saved, but those who have "torn their hearts" in true repentance. But what is true repentance?

There are two words used in the New Testament that are translated in English as *repentance*.

When John the Baptist came preaching in the wilderness, he would cry out to the people, "Repent, for the kingdom of heaven is at hand" (Matthew 4:17). The Greek word for *repent* is *metanoeo*. It is a combination of two Greek words:

meta—meaning "to change," and *noeo*—meaning "the mind." The word literally means "to change the mind, the attitude." This is true repentance. It begins in the heart, the thinking, and is then seen in the outward actions.

But there is another Greek word for *repent* found in the New Testament. This is a word used of Judas when he betrayed Jesus for 30 pieces of silver. This betrayal caused Jesus to be arrested and falsely crucified. He left the betrayal and repented himself and tried to take the silver back to the chief priests and elders and threw it at their feet (Matthew 27:3).

Although what he did is also translated *repent,* it is a different Greek word than John the Baptist used. It is the word *metamelomai.* Again, *meta* means "to change," but *melomai* means "the feelings." This is not a true change of heart or mind.

Although Judas had a change of feelings, he did not have a change of heart. He repented and even wept over what he had done, going through a great emotional upheaval. He even went out and hanged himself for what he had done, but he did not change his heart and admit that Jesus was the Messiah, the One to come.

Judas was a follower, a team member, the accountant, and a friend of Jesus, but he was not a believer. His actions said one thing, but his heart said another. No matter how strong your works may be and how convincing your words are, salvation and true discipleship are an attitude of the heart, not the outward appearance.

It is stated later by the disciples, before the Day of Pentecost, that Judas had gone to "his own place"—meaning hell (Acts 1:25). Judas had a change of emotions, but not a changed life showing a changed heart.

This magnifies what Joel is saying to the citizens of Jerusalem about the upcoming difficult times. Their outward change of action must reflect their change of heart: "Tear your hearts, and not just your clothes. Let your repentance be genuine."

"Turn to the Lord your God: for He is merciful and gracious." Joel says of the Lord, He is merciful and gracious. It does not matter how close the day of wrath may be—if a person will accept the Lord, God will be gracious to that individual.

What is the day of salvation? *Today* is the day of salvation, every single day. Any day is the right day to repent from the heart and turn to God. Right up to the very day of His display of wrath, God will still be gracious to those who call on Him in repentance and faith.

"For He is gracious and merciful." Not only is God gracious, but He is also merciful. Mercy is grace in action. Grace is something God has on the inside of Him—one attribute of His character. But when He displays any of His attributes, it is always in grace, or here called mercy. Mercy is the outward manifestation of God's grace.

God is not only gracious and merciful, but He is also quick to show that grace and mercy to all those who call on Him. Which is what Joel is urging his readers and listeners to do.

"Slow to anger" is also an attribute of God's love for us. He does not send judgment until He has first shown mercy. Many people ask why God allows sin and suffering in the world—why He does not interfere and stamp out all evil and punish all wrongdoers. The most significant reason God is patient is because of His great mercy and grace toward us, His fallen creation.

Slow to anger is the display of His mercy toward us. Because God is slow to anger and great in mercy is why people like Enoch, Noah, Moses, David, and Elijah became the great men of God who made their way into the "Hall of Fame" of Hebrews 11. If God would have acted quickly, none of these would be the heroes they are today.

In fact, if God acted quickly, you would not be here. Each one of us as children of God are glad for His long-suffering toward us today. We want Him to act quickly in anger toward others, but we want grace and patience for ourselves. God is the same toward all mankind—not willing that any should perish, but that all should come to the knowledge of His Son, Jesus.

But it is true: if a person keeps rejecting God's grace and mercy, one day that individual will have to face God's anger as a rejecter of His mercy.

So many nations that God was patient with in history no longer exist because of their attitude toward God's people, Israel. But carnal believers like King Saul and Samson took advantage of God's grace far too long, and God saw to it their lives were taken even though they were believers. They are in heaven now, since they are saints, but they will lose many rewards.

King David was an example of what God can do for a carnal believer when they repent quickly. David lost a newborn child because of his sin of killing Uriah and his adultery with Bathsheba. But David's repentance was deep and heartfelt, filling several of the Psalms, and he went on to be the best king Israel ever had. Aren't you glad God was long-suffering and patient with David? And aren't you glad God has been long-suffering and patient with you?

God is "slow to anger" because He does not send judgment until He has first shown mercy.

Some people ask why God allows sin and suffering in the world and why He doesn't interfere and stamp out evil and punish all wrongdoers. We only need to look at ourselves to realize how much love and patience God really has.

The Bible tells us God relents, or changes His mind, because of evil. What does the Bible mean when it says God changes His mind about evil?

I was on a panel of ministers one day on television, and the question was presented by a local news team to us about this issue. The moderator said, "If God changes His mind, did He do it because He was wrong?" Out of the ten or so ministers, most said God makes mistakes and has to repent.

I felt the blood go to my head. I said, "God is never wrong. When people in the Bible repented, they went from wrong to right and an apology to God was necessary. Because they changed their mind, God changed His mind from His anger and plans for discipline to plans for a blessing. Again, when a person repents to God, they go from wrong to right. When God repents toward those who repent to Him, He changes His mind and goes from right to right.

"It's much like a parent putting down a paddle because the child truly repents for the wrong they have done. The parent was right to plan discipline for the child and then right to forgive them, changing their own mind.

"God is never wrong. He is right for sentencing a person to Hell, but then right to change the sentence to Heaven when the person repents and accepts Jesus as their Lord. The person who repented went from wrong to right, and God went from right to right."

In our passage, Joel exhorts the people of Israel to repent of their evil ways and to turn back to God, who is eager to repent of the evil laid up in store for them because of their disobedience. They change their mind, and so does God.

> 2:14 "Who knows if He will turn and relent, and leave a blessing behind Him—a grain offering and a drink offering for the Lord your God?"

Who knows if God will turn from His anger toward you and repent, replacing His discipline with a blessing? The Hebrew text says, "Who knows when He will return and repent." It is stressing the fact that one day He will return to earth to execute judgment and wrath on those who have rejected Him. But He is also going to pronounce a blessing on those who have accepted Him. On that day He is going to leave a gift on this earth. That gift will be the reinstatement of the meal and drink offering.

This was taught at the beginning of the book. In the day when Joel wrote these words, the priests had omitted this particular ministry to the Lord. As a result, the people were no longer learning about the daily and future plans of God for them. They knew nothing of God's presence and comfort by the Word and the Holy Spirit. Joel pointed out all the calamities that had fallen on them and their nation because of their spiritual decay.

You can be assured of one thing: any natural catastrophe that comes into this earth has a supernatural origin. Evil originates from Satan. And Satan comes against people for two simple reasons: because they are in God's will, and because they are out of God's will.

Being a believer—a Christian today—does not automatically exempt you from attacks of Satan. In fact, it more or less guarantees it! Just as God, in His universal love, sends rain on the just and unjust alike, so Satan, in his universal hatred, visits evil on both the just and the unjust alike.

The only difference between the believer and the unbeliever is that the believer knows he doesn't have to stand for such illegal activity. He takes the sword of the Spirit—the Word of God—and uses the promises against the works of Satan. He knows God will deliver him out of the problems, whether deliverance comes today or in the days to come. "Many are the afflictions of the righteous, but the Lord delivers him out of them *all*" (Psalm 34:19).

The Word is the issue, and patience is the power that takes us from our present day of calamity into the day of deliverance. Jesus spoke to His calamities, such as the storm that came on the boat. The passengers who benefited, seeing a calm sea, were His disciples.

Before the first coming of the Messiah, these offerings were made looking forward to the redemption Jesus would accomplish on the Cross for His people. These were made in anticipation of a future event marking their salvation and security in Christ.

After the first coming of the Lord, these offerings were made in memory of a *past* event marking salvation and security. Of the Communion which teaches the work of the cross, Jesus said, "This do…in *remembrance* of Me. For as often as you eat this bread and drink this cup, you proclaim the Lord's death till He comes" (1 Corinthians 11:25-26). In taking the Lord's Supper, we take part in an offering of giving thanks, remembering with gratitude all that was accomplished for us by our Lord on the Cross of Calvary. We do this until Jesus returns to rule on earth.

Then, during the millennial reign of Christ, the meal and drink offerings will be made to the Lord *again, looking back* to the work of the Cross. The Old Testament offerings looked forward, and our New Testament offerings look back to the source of our completed redemption—the Cross of Jesus.

The curse of spiritual death was removed in the Old Testament by looking *forward* to the death of Messiah on the Cross. The curse of spiritual death is removed today in the New Testament by looking *back* to the death of Jesus on the Cross.

The curse of spiritual death and separation from God is removed because Jesus, the last Adam, went to the Cross and undid what the first Adam had done.

The first tree (on which the forbidden fruit hung) brought mankind into condemnation. The second tree (on which hung our crucified Lord) brought mankind out of condemnation and into life.

It becomes effective in you when you accept Him. His choice was to die for you. Your choice is to receive Him and His work.

This is what we will be commemorating and remembering in the meal and drink offerings. We will do this in the very presence of the King of kings and Lord of lords during His glorious reign on the earth—the King and His family.

5

GOD'S SANCTIFICATION

JOEL 2:15-17

THE GREAT ASSEMBLY

Beginning with verse 15 through the end of chapter 2, Joel discusses the coming millennial kingdom—the 1,000-year rulership of the Lord Jesus Christ. The earth will be occupied by believers only: many in resurrection bodies who return with Jesus at Armageddon, and the rest in natural bodies who were saved and survived the Tribulation.

Two things are taught by the rulership of Jesus on earth. First, Jesus will demonstrate God's intention of what the earth should look like under a rule of righteousness. Second, He will demonstrate that even with His physical presence—with perfect environment, government, weather, riches, health, and world peace—man can still sin without the presence of Satan. This already occurred in the Garden of Eden: two perfect people, living in a perfect world, instructed by God in what to do and what not to do, still sinned.

God's primary message during the Millennium is this: perfect environment is not the answer to humanity's problem. Humankind's nature is the problem. Those in resurrection bodies will not rebel, but those in natural bodies, which still retain the nature of the flesh, will rebel even in perfect environment. The rebellion at the end of the Millennium will be even greater in number than the battle of Armageddon.

> 2:15 "Blow the trumpet in Zion, consecrate a fast, call a sacred assembly:"

"Blow the trumpet." As we have already noted, this word trumpet refers to a literal trumpet, not a ram's horn as in verse 1. That horn was blown by the captains of Israel to sound an alarm of an approaching enemy. In contrast, this trumpet—sounded by the Lord—announces His return to earth at His second and eternal coming.

On this day, Jesus will come back with His army of saints to deliver the children of Israel from destruction at the hands of Satan's army. The trumpet blast is a signal to the Lord's people to come from the four winds and to assemble themselves together in one place, as in the days of old. The regathering of God's people back to Israel will be supernatural and accomplished by the Lord.

"Consecrate [Sanctify] *a fast."* This command to "sanctify" (KJV) a fast indicates that the people of Israel are to repent for their way of living. In Old Testament days, whenever the people were called together for a time of public fasting, it was because they had sinned and turned their backs on the Lord.

Those who are called together to sanctify or consecrate a fast are Jewish believers who knew the Lord was coming but had not lived their lives in righteousness before Him.

"*Call a sacred* [solemn] *assembly.*" This assembly includes all the believers in Israel but specifically refers to those assembling in Jerusalem. This will be the place of Jesus' bodily return as described by Zechariah the prophet:

> Behold, the day of the Lord is coming, and your spoil will be divided in your midst. For I will gather all the nations to battle against Jerusalem; the city shall be taken, the houses rifled, and the women ravished. Half of the city shall go into captivity, but the remnant of the people shall not be cut off from the city. Then the Lord will go forth and fight against those nations, as He fights in the day of battle. And in that day His feet will stand on the Mount of Olives, which faces Jerusalem on the east. And the Mount of Olives shall be split in two, from east to west, making a very large valley; half of the mountain shall move toward the north and half of it toward the south (Zechariah 14:1-4).

Jesus gave a prophetic look at this event when He spoke on the use of faith. When He said, "this mountain," He was speaking of the one He and His disciples were standing on—the Mount of Olives. It will one day be removed and cast into the sea (Mark 11:23). The valley that opens up will be created by the splitting of that mountain. Jesus will then walk through the eastern gate into the city of Jerusalem and set up His throne in the temple to rule over all nations for 1,000 years.

> 2:16 "Gather the people, sanctify the congregation, assemble the elders, gather the children and nursing babes; let the bridegroom go out from his chamber, and the bride from her dressing room."

"*Gather the people.*" The first event after Jesus sets up His earthly kingdom will be the assembling of the people together. Who will go forth and gather them? The Lord Himself gave us the answer in Matthew 24:29-31:

> Immediately after the tribulation of those days, the sun will be darkened, and the moon will not give its light; the stars will fall from heaven, and the powers of the heavens will be shaken. Then the sign of the Son of Man will appear in heaven, and then all the tribes of the earth will mourn, and they will see the Son of Man coming on the clouds of heaven with power and great glory. And He will send His angels with a great sound of a trumpet, and they will gather together His elect from the four winds, from one end of heaven to the other.

The people will be gathered together by God's angels at the command of Jesus.

"*Sanctify the congregation.*" How will this great congregation of people, gathered "from the four winds," be sanctified? Simple: the unbelievers will be removed, leaving behind only the believers. Jesus foretold this in Matthew 25:31-33,46:

> When the Son of Man comes in His glory, and all the holy angels with Him, then He will sit on the throne of His glory. All the nations will be gathered before Him, and He will separate them one from another, as

> a shepherd divides his sheep [believers] from the goats [unbelievers]. And He will set the sheep on His right hand, but the goats on the left.... And these [on the left] will go away into everlasting punishment, but the righteous into eternal life.

John the Baptist also foresaw this day when he said of Jesus,

> I indeed baptize you with water unto repentance, but He who is coming after me is mightier than I, whose sandals I am not worthy to carry. He will baptize you with the Holy Spirit [believers] and fire [unbelievers]. His winnowing fan is in His hand, and He will thoroughly clean out His threshing floor, and gather His wheat [believers] into the barn; but He will burn up the chaff [unbelievers] with unquenchable fire (Matthew 3:11-12).

Returning now to Joel 2:16:

"*Assemble the elders.*" The elders spoken of here are not priests who minister before the Lord, but the leaders of the land—the kings, presidents, and governors who held authority over Israel. These too are to be gathered with the congregation in the great assembly hosted by the Lord Himself. And what an assembly it will be!

"*Gather the children.*" The Hebrew word here refers to school-age children. On that day there will be no school (I imagine the kids will love that day!). They too will be gathered with the congregation and the elders in the great assembly of believers.

"And nursing babes." These are the newborns, the very young who are not yet weaned. They too will be part of that great assembly, reminding us of our Lord's words: "Let the little children to come to Me, and do not forbid them; for of such is the kingdom of heaven" (Matthew 19:14).

The Coming of the Royal Couple

"Let the bridegroom go out from his chamber, and the bride from her dressing room." Who is the bride? This is the Church of Jesus Christ, from the Day of Pentecost to the Rapture of the Church. These are the tens of billions of saints who will accompany the Lord on His triumphant return to the earth! We will be revealed to the world as Jesus' bride. The closet door will be opened, and the mystery of the Church will be openly displayed.

The apostle John had a vision of this glorious day—the return of the Royal Couple. Jesus, the Bridegroom, and the Church, the bride, are riding on white horses and dressed in white robes. Jesus alone will fight the battle and defeat the armies of the world. After the victory, He will present the Bride to all the inhabitants of the earth.

> Let us be glad and rejoice and give Him glory, for the marriage of the Lamb has come, and His wife has made herself ready. And to her it was granted to be arrayed in fine linen, clean and bright, for the fine linen is the righteous acts of the saints. Then he [the angel] said to me, "Write: 'Blessed are those who are called to the marriage supper of the Lamb!'" And he said to me, "These are the true sayings of God" (Revelation 19:7-9).

> Now I saw heaven opened, and behold, a white horse. And He who sat on him was called Faithful and True, and in righteousness He judges and makes war. His eyes were like a flame of fire, and on His head were many crowns. He had a name written that no one knew except Himself. He was clothed with a robe dipped in blood, and His name is called The Word of God. And the armies in heaven, clothed in fine linen, white and clean, followed Him on white horses. Now out of His mouth goes a sharp sword, that with it He should strike the nations. And He Himself will rule them with a rod of iron. He Himself treads the winepress of the fierceness and wrath of Almighty God. And He has on His robe and on His thigh a name written: KING OF KINGS AND LORD OF LORDS (Revelation 19:11-16).

As Jesus returns with His bride, He will first declare war on the armies coming against Jerusalem. He will fight alone. The Bride will remain in the sky with the angels and watch the Groom—the Lord Jesus—destroy the armies with the words of His mouth. After the battle, the wedding plans will be made while the Groom prepares to judge the nations, separating the believers from the unbelievers. After judging, and removing the unbelievers from the earth, the marriage supper will begin. The earth will then enter not only the 1,000-year reign of Jesus but also a 1,000-year honeymoon for the Royal Couple. Even Buckingham Palace cannot compare to this.

> 2:17 "Let the priests, who minister to the Lord, weep between the porch and the altar; let them say, 'Spare

Your people, O Lord, and do not give Your heritage to reproach, that the nations should rule over them. Why should they say among the peoples, "Where is their God?"'"

Why should the ministers of the Lord weep? Because they have failed in their responsibility of instructing the people in the Word and the ways of God. They were to be the link between the people and the Lord, but they had not been faithful to fulfill their ministry, and they failed in their sacred responsibility as intercessors between the Lord and His people. They must weep not only for the sins of the people but also for their own sins in order to fulfill their priestly duty.

They are to weep "between the porch and the altar." The porch is the place where the people bore the responsibility to learn the ways of the Lord. The altar is the place of sacrifice and offerings to the Lord. The priests had failed in their responsibility to teach at the porch what they practiced at the altar. Repentance must begin at the house of God before the people can truly change.

Another part of the priest's ministry is to cry to the Lord for mercy—to save (spare) the people. This is truly part of the ministry of intercession. Like Moses, these men were to put God in remembrance of His promises to His people and intercede with tears for the sinful nation. God tells them that because of their laxness in fulfilling their duty, they were helping to turn the people over to their enemies.

This is the duty and calling of an intercessor: to put God in remembrance of His Word and His grace. The priests should have been reminding God that "he who touches you touches the apple of His eye" (Zechariah 2:8).

So the priests and ministers of the Lord are commanded to intercede on behalf of the people. And as we will see in the coming verses, the Lord is quick to hear and respond. He is waiting to pour out His blessings on His people.

6

BLESSINGS OF THE KINGDOM

JOEL 2:18-22

SUMMARY OF BLESSINGS

Beginning with Joel 2:18, Joel foretells what is going to happen after the Lord has returned to earth in power and great glory to set up His kingdom. Jesus will have rescued Israel from her foes. From there to the end of chapter 2, we find Joel's prophecy of the millennial reign of Christ. In these verses, Joel describes some of the blessings the Lord will begin pouring out on Israel, His land.

The following list reveals all the blessings of the Millennium and their scriptural references first. Then, in the next two chapters of this book, we go back and examine in detail the individual blessings told by Joel in prophecy.

1. Satan and the demons will be bound in hell (Revelation 20:1-30).

2. Satan's followers will be taken from the earth (Matthew 13:41-43; 25:31-46).
3. The Holy Spirit will be poured out on all flesh (Isaiah 32:15; Ezekiel 39:29).
4. The knowledge of the glory of the Lord will cover all the earth (Habakkuk 2:14).
5. There will be no more war (Isaiah 2:4; Psalm 46:9).
6. The whole earth will break forth in praise to God (Isaiah 14:7).
7. There will be a population explosion to replenish the earth (Ezekiel 36:38).
8. There will be no more thorns or thistles (Isaiah 32:13,15).
9. The nature of animals will be changed and tamed to live in harmony together (Isaiah 11:6,9).
10. No more drought with plenty of rain and sunshine, perfect climate (Isaiah 30:26; 32:15; 35:6-7).
11. There will be abundance of crops (Amos 9:13; Psalm 72:16).
12. The desert will bloom (Isaiah 35:1).
13. There will be universal prosperity (Micah 4:4).
14. Longevity will be restored, and death will be banished, except for crimes of capital punishment.

What a wonderful time it will be during the Millennium! Now, let's look at Joel's prophetic vision of those glorious days.

The Lord's Response

> 2:18 "Then the Lord will be zealous for His land, and pity His people."

"Then the Lord will be zealous...and pity." Our God has emotions and cares for people, especially His own. Whenever anyone speaks evil of the church of Jesus Christ, God rises in anger. Jesus went through crucifixion and shed His blood to create the church. God rises in anger to protect His people and stop those who speak evil of the church and wish to destroy it.

Although God can become jealous, envious, loving, and more, His emotions are always holy. God's anger is never a sin, nor is His jealousy evil. Since we are created in His image and He has emotions, we can identify with His attitude and feelings toward iniquity and His protection of His own. This is how we feel toward our own children when they are ridiculed or put in evil situations. The Bible is clear that God is not a man, but much of our being is created in His image. Our feelings of anger toward iniquity and injustice in the world help us understand God. God used Himself as a pattern when He created Adam and Eve.

> 2:19 "The Lord will answer and say to His people, 'Behold, I will send you grain and new wine and oil, and you will be satisfied by them; I will no longer make you a reproach among the nations.'"

"I will no more make you a reproach among the nations." In the millennial reign of our Lord Jesus, He will redeem the time Israel has been under the feet of other nations who have abused the Jewish people through the centuries. Since the days of Abraham, the children of Israel have had great prosperity and favor among other nations. But since Satan is the god of this world and he hates Israel, his anger and jealousy of the

Jewish people have begun many wars and led to long periods of slavery for them. Some are recorded in the Bible and others recorded in history.

They were held in slavery in Egypt, ransacked by the Assyrians, taken captive by the Babylonians, conquered and subjugated by the Romans, and persecuted and scattered throughout the nations of the world since the time of the Romans. Yet whenever they have gone into captivity and persecution, a remnant has always remained faithful to the God of Abraham, Isaac, and Jacob during their persecution. And the Lord is going to reward that faithfulness. He will keep His Word to the Jewish people and fulfill every promise made to Abraham and his descendants.

One of those promises is *full* possession of the land of Canaan. The nation of Israel has never fully possessed the land promised to them by the Lord. The closest they ever came was during the reign of Solomon, but even that did not last long. During the millennial reign of Jesus, however, the Lord will give Israel the land He promised them in total. He is going to fulfill all the covenants between Himself and His chosen people. That will be the time when Israel will enter the period of the greatest prosperity her people have ever known.

Today we are seeing the Jews returning to their native land. Little by little, they are restoring the barren wasteland to its former splendor. But what is happening today is small in comparison to what the Lord will do for them when He brings them back to their long-promised homeland. That is when the desert will blossom with vegetation, as every prophecy and promise regarding their land of milk and honey is fulfilled.

When the event surrounding the presentation of all the land promised to Israel takes place, it will be supernatural. No nation or group of nations (United Nations) can claim credit. It will come through one Person—the world's Messiah, the Lord Jesus Christ.

"I will send you corn, and wine, and oil, and you will be satisfied with it." This promise means Israel will be more prosperous than they have ever been or could have imagined.

In our present age, we measure prosperity financially—in terms of currency in the bank, net worth, investments, and real estate holdings. But in the day of the writing of this prophecy to Israel, it was estimated differently. In an agricultural economy like that of Israel in Joel's day, prosperity was measured by productive vineyards, bumper crops of grain, fruitful orchards, and increasing flocks and herds. So, when Joel speaks of the Lord satisfying His people with grain, wine, and oil, he was prophesying that the millennial reign of Jesus Christ will be a period of unparalleled abundance and prosperity.

THE LORD FIGHTS FOR ISRAEL

> 2:20 "But I will remove far from you the northern army, and will drive him away into a barren and desolate land, with his face toward the eastern sea and his back toward the western sea; his stench will come up, and his foul odor will rise because he has done monstrous things."

"I will remove far from you the northern army, and will drive him away into a barren and desolate land." This verse foretells the battle of Armageddon. The "northern army," which will descend on Israel to surround and destroy its army and

people, will enter the nation through the Valley of Megiddo. The only access to this valley is from the north. The southern end opens onto the Plain of Megiddo, in front of the city of Jerusalem. It will be a natural corridor of attack. It will be on this plain that Jesus Christ Himself will meet and destroy the armies of the world in the greatest battle of all time. The Lord will come back to earth with His saints and angels to rescue Israel. He will drive the northern army back into a barren and desolate place. This will also be an easy place for Jesus Christ, one Man, to destroy all the armies of the world.

"*With his face toward the eastern sea and his back toward the western sea.*" The "eastern sea" is the Dead Sea, and the "western sea" is the Mediterranean. These events are also prophesied in Daniel 11:44-45, which says of the coming antichrist: "But news out of the east and north shall trouble him; therefore he shall go out with great fury to destroy and annihilate many. And he shall plant the tents of his palace between the seas and the glorious holy mountain; yet he shall come to his end, and no one will help him."

Notice that "seas" is plural—a reference to the Dead Sea and the Mediterranean Sea. This is the place where the antichrist will come to his end, as he is killed by the Lord Jesus between these two seas.

We have also seen that the prophet Zechariah foretells these end-time events, prophesying in chapter 14 that, at His return to earth, Jesus will set His feet on the Mount of Olives, which will split in two by a great earthquake at His coming. "And in that day it shall be that living waters will flow from Jerusalem, half of them toward the eastern sea and half of them toward the western sea. In both summer and winter it shall occur" (Zechariah 14:8). The "living waters" will come from the Mount of Olives. As the feet of Jesus touch the mountaintop, it will split in two and water will flow out. This will be a literal fulfillment of Mark 11:23-24, where Jesus said His disciples could speak to this mountain (Olives) to be removed and cast into the sea, and it would obey them.

When the great army of the antichrist is defeated, the Mount of Olives will split in two by a giant earthquake, and the waters of two great seas will flow together. As a result, the Dead Sea will become a body of fresh water, and God will restore it to life. From then on, there will be "living water" to bring life back to this dead area of the world (Ezekiel 47:1-10).

Because God Kept His Word Before, He Will Keep It Again

> 2:21 "Fear not, O land; be glad and rejoice, for the Lord has done marvelous things!"

What God was about to do for Israel was not something new. God had performed miracles from Israel's earliest days with Abraham to the day He will deliver them from the evil armies coming to destroy them at Armageddon. "...forget not all His benefits" (Psalm 103:2) is a reminder that not only can Scripture give us hope for today but remembering how God brought us through seemingly impossible situations before can bring us faith to stand against the problems we are yet to face.

We often remember our failings, but choosing to remember our successes can bring more success. Hebrews chapters 3 and 4 tell the Jews to remember Meribah, a place of no water, yet God miraculously provided a flood of water from a rock. He did not do this once, but twice—once for each wilderness generation. In other words, what God has done before, He can do again.

Why should we worry about a lack of food when a shortage or famine is looming? Has God lost the recipe for manna? Can He still split a sea? Can He still multiply loaves and fishes—twice? Why do we have Communion services so often? It is so we can "do this in remembrance" of Jesus' sacrifice on the Cross that saved us. How many times did Jesus ask His disciples, "Don't you remember?"

It is good to keep a ledger of God's miracles in your life and pull it out when you are facing a seemingly impossible problem. You will have to laugh when you remember God has brought you through worse problems than this.

Israel will remember God's past miracles, which not only created the nation of Israel but kept it for centuries. The God who also kept His nation and His people will do so forever. Israel is the only everlasting nation on earth.

Abraham met Melchisedec, the priest of God, at Salem (Jerusalem) in Genesis 14. Has it ever crossed your mind that Jerusalem already existed when Abraham met Melchisedec? We are not told when the city began, and it will last forever as the New Jerusalem and as a throne for the Lord Jesus. If God created Jerusalem sometime in ages past and protected it from its enemies throughout history, He will continue to do so into eternity.

Israel was overrun by other nations after its invasion in AD 70 and remained occupied by its enemies for more than 2,000 years. It became a nation again for the Jews in 1948. God keeps His Word no matter how long it takes. He will do the same for Israel at the battle of Armageddon, and He will keep His Word to you every day. God did it before, and He will do it again. He has done marvelous things.

> 2:22 "Do not be afraid you beasts of the field; for the open pastures are springing up, and the tree bears its fruit; the fig tree and vine yield their strength."

God does not forget the necessities of life when He delivers us. What good would it do for God to deliver Israel at Armageddon and then not replenish the cattle and crops? After Armageddon is over—the battle to end all battles—the landscape will look like a barren wasteland. The problem is it will be a barren wasteland. But God tells Israel now that He has already planned to replace and replenish everything. The people will not even have to think about anything.

In your life, God will not only fix your problems but also fix all the problems your problem created. He always does "exceedingly, abundantly above all that we ask or think" (Ephesians 3:20). God never forgets the "little things" when He corrects the "big things."

Israel will blossom and bloom during the Millennium, and it begins right after the battle of Armageddon. Evil men and armies cannot create something God cannot fix.

7

THE OUTPOURING OF GOD'S SPIRIT

JOEL 2:23-32

In Chapter 6 we looked at the return of the Lord Jesus and the establishing of His millennial kingdom. In that day, He will begin to pour out His blessings on *all* believers—on *all* flesh.

Now, in this chapter, we continue to examine the same outpouring of blessings, but from a different aspect. From Joel 2:23 through the end of chapter 2, we will consider the physical results that will come about as a result of God's outpouring of His Holy Spirit on all flesh.

I keep emphasizing all flesh because it did not begin that way. The Day of Pentecost saw 120 disciples filled with the Holy Spirit in the upper room at Jerusalem. This, by no means, was *all* flesh. By the time the end of the day had come, 3,000 more people accepted Jesus and were probably filled with the Holy Spirit also. But again, that was by no means *all* flesh. *All* flesh would mean exactly that—*every person*—which would include unbelievers.

Through the centuries, many who were saved have also received the Holy Spirit's filling and spoken with tongues, as they did in Acts chapters 2, 8, 10, and 19. This outpouring of the Holy Spirit began at the opening of the Church Age and has occurred daily in the lives of those receiving salvation and moving into discipleship. During times of revival, being filled with the Holy Spirit and speaking with tongues has accompanied the great revivals of history.

But how could Acts 2 and other occurrences in Acts have been for *all* flesh? There have always been more unbelievers on the earth than believers (Matthew 7:13-14). It is because Peter gave Joel's prophecy of the outpouring of the Holy Spirit as beginning in "the last days" (Acts 2:17).

The last days do not begin at the beginning of the tribulation or Millennium; they began on the Day of Pentecost. Since then, the Holy Spirit has always been poured out only on believers.

But on the day the Millennium begins, all people on earth will be believers. All unbelievers will have been removed and sentenced to hell with Satan, demons, fallen angels, the antichrist, the false prophet, the beast, and all rejecters of Jesus from all times.

So, grasp this fact: ***we are in the last days now.*** The last days began on the Day of Pentecost and continue through today, through the Tribulation, and into the second coming of Jesus to destroy the antichrist and remove all unbelievers from the earth.

To repeat what I just said: when the Holy Spirit is poured out as Jesus begins the kingdom reign, it will be on *all* people—*all* flesh—because there will be no sinners on earth on that day. Later in the Millennium, there will be unbelievers, because even in a time of perfect environment with Jesus on the throne, many will reject Him. They will be born from parents who were saved during the Tribulation, endured through it, and entered the Millennium. They will have children during the Millennium, but the children will not accept Jesus. A large group, which cannot even be counted, will rise up against Him at the end of the Millennium and try to overthrow Him (Revelation 20:7-10). They will be sentenced to the lake of fire with Satan and all who rejected Jesus in all time periods.

THE FORMER AND LATTER RAIN

> 2:23 "Be glad then, you children of Zion, and rejoice in the Lord your God; for He has given you the former rain faithfully, and He will cause the rain to come down for you—the former rain, and the latter rain in the first month."

In the agricultural economy of ancient Israel, the "former rain" and the "latter rain" were important times in the harvest of crops. The former rain was the predictable, moderate spring rain which came at planting time each season to provide the necessary moisture to cause the seeds to germinate and begin to grow the eventual crop. The latter autumn rain provided the abundant, large amounts of water needed for harvesting the great number of crops. Both—the former and latter rains—could usually be counted on to arrive regularly.

In our time, I can well remember when our weather was more stable and predictable than it is today. In recent years, it seems the world's climatic conditions have become so erratic, no one can safely say what is likely to occur. Weather forecasters everywhere point out the difficulty of anticipating our constantly changing weather conditions. Recent tornadoes and hurricanes are more plentiful and powerful and are striking places never bothered before. As a result of prolonged droughts and repeated crop failures, wide-scale famine is a topic of much concern among world leaders. Increasingly, it is being predicted that worldwide food and water shortages are possible.

Yet, we as Christians are assured of our future. We know from the pages of God's Word there is coming a day when all of this will be corrected again. This is what Joel is saying in these verses. The former and latter rains can be counted on with the same regularity as the coming of the Holy Spirit. The heavens and the earth will again work with regularity and perfect order.

But this passage has a spiritual meaning, because you and I are now living close to the time of the coming latter rain of the Holy Spirit. It will begin pouring in abundance at the end of the Church Age, continue through the time of the Tribulation, and be given in even greater abundance at the beginning of the Millennium. So much power and presence of the Holy Spirit will be given at the beginning of the Millennium, it will be like both the former and the latter rain occurring in the same month. The former rain is the presence and power of the Holy Spirit in the Old Testament. The latter rain is the presence of the Holy Spirit in the New Testament. The presence of the Lord at the beginning of the Millennium will be greater because no unbelievers will be on the earth. They will have been removed after Jesus comes to earth and sentenced to hell until the Millennium is over.

Paul gives the millennial reign of Jesus the title, "the dispensation of the fullness of the times" (Ephesians 1:10). It combines the best—and more—of all the time periods before, including the former and latter rain: a double outpouring of the Holy Spirit on all the inhabitants of the earth.

Jesus told His disciples, and us, the purpose of the Holy Spirit's coming to fill us is to give us divine power to witness, win souls to Jesus, and take the message of the gospel to the world (Acts 1:8).

Witnessing is not natural, a formula, or a memorized method—it is supernatural. It takes the receiving of divine power and the use of our prayer language, tongues, to prepare us to properly witness. I believe it is important to depend on the Holy Spirit for divine guidance and wisdom to lead a person to salvation.

One of the gifts of the Holy Spirit is a word of knowledge. Jesus used this gift often when He witnessed. He told Nathaniel, "I saw you sitting under a tree." Nathaniel replied, "You are the Son of God" (John 1:48-50). Jesus told the woman at the well, "You have had five husbands, and the one you are living with now is not your husband." She told Jesus she perceived He was a prophet (John 4:16-19).

I once sat next to a young man on a plane, and the Holy Spirit said to me, "He is ready to receive Me." The young man told me he had been shown how to become a Christian by a friend weeks before but had forgotten how. He had prayed that morning for someone to explain it to him, and he sat next to me. I led him to Jesus immediately. It was an example of supernatural leading to win a soul. The Holy Spirit's main ministry is to equip us and empower us for witnessing (Acts 1:8).

> 2:24 "The threshing floors shall be full of wheat, and the vats shall overflow with new wine and oil."

These verses not only speak of the abundance of grain for food and wine for rejoicing, but also of spiritual food in abundance—the knowledge of the glory of the Lord revealed in all the world. God never gives just a small amount of anything. He gives everlasting life, the Holy Spirit to overflowing, joy unspeakable and full of glory, and the knowledge of God's glory will also be overflowing, like the seas that cover the earth (Habakkuk 2:14).

We think we have seen manifestations of the presence of the Holy Spirit in our day, but each one is nothing compared to the supernatural presence of the Holy Spirit that will be manifested on the day our Lord returns to rule and reign over the entire planet. All the unbelievers will be removed, so only believers remain. And each believer will be filled to overflowing with the Spirit of God! The whole earth will be filled with praise and worship to the Lord, and it will go on for 1,000 years. His kingdom will have come, and His desires will be accomplished on earth as it is in heaven.

And the good news is that we as Christians do not have to wait for that day to begin living in the blessings and fullness of God's Spirit. The latter rain began on the Day of Pentecost and never stopped. The Church of Jesus Christ should be receiving similar benefits today as we will enjoy in the millennial reign of Jesus Christ.

The Millennium will be a period of universal prosperity—a time when the former and latter rains will arrive at the same time and without measure. Prosperity will be the order of the day. But even material prosperity will be just a picture of what is happening spiritually. The material and spiritual worlds are closely linked. This is why the apostle John said, "Beloved, I pray that you may prosper in all things and be in health, just as your soul prospers" (3 John 2). John knew that outward, material prosperity in the life of a spiritual believer is only a manifestation of inward, spiritual prosperity.

God's prosperity does not originate in the pocketbook but by His will and in the spirit. It does not depend on what is in the wallet, purse, or bank, but on what is in the heart. Jesus said, "A good man out of the good treasure of his heart brings forth good things..." (Matthew 12:35).

The Restoration of Israel

> 2:25 "So I will restore to you the years that the swarming locust [Assyrians] has eaten, the crawling locust [Babylonians], the consuming locust [Romans], and the chewing locust [Armageddon], my great army which I sent among you."

God is not referring to the four physical locust invasions the nation has experienced, but the four corresponding military invasions of Israel—two in the Old Testament and two in the New Testament. The last one will be the battle of Armageddon, from which God will save Israel from all the armies gathered together from all the nations of the world. The Millennium will truly be the greatest case of cursing turned into blessing. Israel and Jerusalem will no longer be the target of Satan and all nations of the world.

Jesus said of the coming Tribulation that the Jewish nation and people will be hated of *all nations* because of the name of Jesus. The entire nation of Israel and its property will again belong to the Jewish people. And Jesus Himself will rule from the temple in Jerusalem forever. In that time, and forever after that time, Israel will possess the entire Promised Land. The closest Israel ever came to owning all of the land promised to them was under the reign of Solomon.

But there is coming a time when the Jews will own all the land from the Mediterranean Sea to the Tigris and Euphrates Rivers, including areas now occupied by their enemies. All this territory will one day be restored to Israel, just as the Lord Jesus promised. That is the time when all prophecies concerning the ownership of land for Israel and the Jews will be fulfilled—the Abrahamic Covenant.

Today, some well-meaning Christians and political believers speak of trying to return Israel to its rightful land. God was behind the United Nations act of 1948 when Israel was given their land. But the land will never be given totally until Jesus returns. No government, politician, Christian minister, or pastor will accomplish it. It will be done by Jesus personally at His second coming, when every nation will see Him, every knee will bow, and every tongue will confess that Jesus Christ is King of kings and Lord of lords.

ASSURANCE OF GOD'S ABUNDANCE AND HIS PRESENCE

> 2:26 "You shall eat in plenty and be satisfied, and praise the name of the Lord your God, who has dealt wondrously with you; and My people shall never be put to shame."

"You shall eat in plenty and be satisfied." In the time of the Millennium there is going to be plenty of food. No one will go hungry. Everyone will be fully satisfied. Hunger will be a thing of the past.

"You shall...praise the name of the Lord your God, who has dealt wondrously with you." In those days, praise will be universal. The whole earth will be full of praise. People everywhere will continually praise God for the wondrous way He has provided for His people.

"*And My people shall never be put to shame* [disappointed]." During the glorious reign of the Lord Jesus, not one of God's people will ever again suffer disappointment from lies or broken promises.

David said, looking back at the end of his life, "I have been young, and now am old; yet I have not seen the righteous forsaken, nor his descendants begging bread" (Psalm 37:25). David also said, "The Lord knows the days of the upright, and their inheritance shall be forever. They shall not be ashamed in the evil time, and in the days of famine they shall be satisfied" (Psalm 37:18-19).

These promises were not only true for David and his descendants, but for us today also. Most of all, this is true for the entire nation David ruled over—Israel.

It is one thing to *believe* in God's faithfulness, to proclaim and say it because it is in God's Word—it is quite another thing to *know* God's faithfulness, to have proven it by personal experience. Faith is wonderful; the Bible tells us we must have faith in God if we are to please Him (Hebrews 11:6). But how much greater is that faith when we know the One in whom we place our faith. It is good to know that God can meet our need, and even greater to know God has met our need. We know that He has come through before, and it is even greater to know He will do it again. Faith in the Lord comes much easier when you know His track record—personally.

The only way to gain personal experience with God's faithfulness is by stepping out in faith to begin with. The first step in trusting God should begin a long road of experiencing trust in God. It is impossible to be disappointed by standing on a promise of God from His Word. God has to uphold His Word. It cannot return to Him void; it must prosper in what He sent it to accomplish (Isaiah 55:11).

To prosper in life, like God, we must have our priorities in line with His. God's greatest creation is His Word. He has placed it above His own name—His reputation. In the Word, God says the greatest use of prosperity is to use it to proclaim the gospel. Not only do we witness, but we also help those who are called to go into all the world—missionaries and mission organizations.

Many men and women contributed to Jesus' ministry, and in Acts many people contributed to the ministries of Paul, Barnabas, Mark, Peter, and others. Their successes became the successes of all who gave to their ministries. We not only make the ministry to others our own priority by our giving, but the ministry to the world also becomes a team effort that includes us as part of the team. Again, the highest priority of a desire to prosper is to give into the ministry of soulwinning: "...it is He who gives you power to get wealth, that He may establish His covenant which He swore to your fathers..." (Deuteronomy 8:18).

Prosperity can be used for other things—the desires and necessities of life—but these are the remaining baskets of bread to take home after the multitudes have been fed.

> 2:27 "Then you shall know that I am in the midst of Israel: I am the Lord your God and there is no other. My people shall never be put to shame."

"Then you shall know that I am in the midst of Israel." Why will the people of Israel know that God is in their midst? Because in that day their knowledge of Him will no longer be by faith only, but by actual sight. God is telling His people, "You have always known by faith that I have been with you, but on that day you will also know because you will see Me with your eyes. Faith will have become sight."

"Then you shall know that...I am the Lord your God, and there is no other. My people shall never be put to shame." Once again, the Lord assures us that in that day His people will never be disappointed. What blessed assurance, and what comfort and joy to know that God always will be with us. But until that day, when sight will accompany our faith, we still live by faith. We may not see Jesus right now with our eyes, but we understand we do not live by sight today—we continue to walk by faith, "seeing what cannot be seen."

THE OUTPOURING OF THE SPIRIT

> 2:28 "And it shall come to pass afterward that I will pour out My Spirit on all flesh; your sons and your daughters shall prophesy, your old men shall dream dreams, your young men shall see visions."

"And it shall come to pass afterward, that I will pour out My Spirit." When is "afterward?" After what? After the second coming—the second advent of the Lord Jesus Christ. After He has come from heaven, returned to earth, established His kingdom, removed all unbelievers, sanctified and rewarded those who made it through the Tribulation, and entered His millennial reign. Then the Holy Spirit will be poured out on *all* flesh. And unlike the Day of Pentecost, where the outpouring began with 120 believers in a city containing many more unbelievers, the day of Jesus' return to rule the earth will see the Holy Spirit poured out only on believers. Again, there will be no unbelievers on earth—they were removed before the thousand-year reign of Jesus began.

But what else makes the outpouring of the Holy Spirit in Peter's day different from the outpouring when Jesus comes to reign? The Holy Spirit's appearance at Pentecost was not the first pouring out, but the second. The future outpouring at Jesus' return to earth to reign will be the third outpouring.

The Holy Spirit's outpouring in the Old Testament was referred to by Joel as the former rain. Remember, in the opening chapters this was a smaller rain for the planting of crops. The second rain, referred to as the latter rain, began on the Day of Pentecost and was a deluge compared to the Old

Testament—the former outpouring. This second rain was recognized by the farmers as the more abundant rain before the crop was harvested, to ensure a large harvest.

The outpouring of the Holy Spirit at the return of Jesus to rule the earth will be a combination of the former (Old Testament outpouring) and latter (New Testament outpouring) rain. And it will be poured out on *all* flesh, *all* at once (Joel 2:23). Because the world will only be occupied with believers, the Holy Spirit will fall on all humanity—all flesh. The world has never seen such a day of the combined glory of God poured out on the inhabitants of the earth all at once—those from the Old Testament and those from the New Testament, the Church.

When Peter quoted this verse in Acts 2:16-18, he called the Church Age the last days. To be honest, the last days are not only ahead but have also already begun and have continued for more than 2,000 years. We are in the final days of the last days. Paul confirmed the New Testament age of the Church to be the "last days" in Hebrews 1:2: "has in these last days spoken to us by His Son...."

Joel's prophecy began to be fulfilled on the Day of Pentecost and has been being fulfilled ever since. It will only be totally fulfilled on the day the Lord Jesus returns. Peter's "last days" is a picture of Joel's "afterward." Since everyone on earth will be a child of God, God can pour out His Spirit on "all flesh." Peter took Joel's prophecy and applied it to the beginning of its fulfillment. Joel foresaw and emphasized the end—the completion and fulfillment.

> 2:29 "And also on My menservants and on My maidservants I will pour out My Spirit in those days."

In the Millennium, sons and daughters will prophesy. But this began in the book of Acts. Ananias, a servant in the local church, prophesied to Saul of Tarsus of his future ministry (Acts 9:10-16). Ananias was not a prophet, just a *certain* disciple. Philip's four daughters prophesied (Acts 21:8-9). Women were not used before this time to give prophetic words. Joel's prophecy was being fulfilled.

Servants and handmaids would receive the Holy Spirit—not only kings or prophets. First Corinthians 12 lists the gifts of the Holy Spirit, and both men and women, young and old, could be used by God. We look on the outward appearance, but God looks on the heart. Isn't it good to know that ours is an "equal opportunity" God?

Then the End Shall Come

> 2:30 "And I will show wonders in the heavens and in the earth: blood and fire and pillars of smoke."

"And I will show wonders in the heavens and in the earth: blood and fire and pillars of smoke." From Joel 2:30 on to the end of chapter 2, Joel tells us the signs of the coming battle, the return of the Lord, and the millennial reign of Jesus.

The blood speaks of the battle of Armageddon. The fire represents the outpouring of God's wrath, which will destroy all armies coming against the Lord, the people, and the city of Jerusalem. This is also a reference to the prophecy of John the Baptist: that the wheat (believers) will be gathered and put into the garner (Millennium), while the chaff (unbelievers) will be burned up with unquenchable fire (cast into hell).

The pillars of smoke are a picture of the scene after the devastation of the battle of Armageddon, in which Jesus will destroy all the armies with the brightness of His coming.

> 2:31 "The sun shall be turned into darkness, and the moon into blood, before the coming of the great and awesome day of the Lord."

"The sun shall be turned into darkness, and the moon into blood." Everything I have studied about this verse indicates these events will occur as a result of the battle of Armageddon itself. The pillars of dust and smoke rising from the battleground will literally veil the sun from view and make the moon appear as red as blood.

In these last verses, Joel is preparing us for chapter 3. Here Joel describes in more detail the battle of Armageddon and the return of the Lord.

> 2:32 "And it shall come to pass that whoever calls on the name of the Lord shall be saved. For in Mount Zion and in Jerusalem there shall be deliverance, as the Lord has said, among the remnant whom the Lord calls."

"Whoever calls on the name of the Lord shall be saved." This part of the verse must be interpreted in connection with verse 31, "Before the great and terrible day of the Lord" (KJV). Joel is teaching us that anyone who calls on the Lord before Jesus returns to earth will be saved. But when Jesus makes His final appearance, it will be too late for repentance. That is one reason the day is called "the great and terrible day of

the Lord." It will be great for the believers, but terrible for the unbelievers—those who are in rebellion against the Lord.

"For in Mount Zion and in Jerusalem there shall be deliverance, as the Lord has said, among the remnant whom the Lord calls." Jesus will appear to deliver His people Israel from their enemies. One Man—Jesus—will kill all the millions of soldiers and destroy all the armament and motorized vehicles they have brought into Israel. He will preserve for Himself a remnant of people, those who have put their faith and trust in Him. They will all go into the millennial reign with Jesus, along with saints from all ages.

8

PREPARE FOR BATTLE

JOEL 3:1-10

In the third chapter of his book, Joel tells of the battle of Armageddon and the judgment that will follow. Chapter 2 told the battle from the viewpoint of the inhabitants inside the city of Jerusalem. Chapter 3 tells of the battle as seen by the approaching armies outside the city.

First, Joel describes how the Lord will gather His enemies together for one last climactic confrontation. Then, after the battle, Joel reveals how the Lord will assemble all nations before Him and judge them. This will be the time spoken of by our Lord Jesus in Matthew 25:31-46, when He will separate the sheep (believers) from the goats (unbelievers) from all the nations on earth. The goats will be cast into outer darkness, into everlasting punishment, but the sheep will go into the kingdom—the millennial reign of the Lord Jesus.

Israel's Captivity Ends

> 3:1 "For behold, in those days and at that time, when I bring back the captives of Judah and Jerusalem,"

"For, behold, in those days, and in that time." The term "in those days" refers to the end of the tribulation. "At that time" refers to the second coming of the Lord—His final and eternal return to earth.

"When I bring back the captives of Judah and Jerusalem." This is a poor translation. The Hebrew text says, "When I restore again *the fortunes* of Judah and Jerusalem."

This same idea was expressed in Joel 2:25 where the Lord said, "And I will restore to you the years the swarming locust has eaten, the crawling locust, the consuming locust, and the chewing locust, the great army which I sent among you." These were four military invasions into Israel whose armies stole from the temple treasury and left Israel bankrupt. Israel's inhabitants have been robbed, taken into slavery, murdered, and scattered through the years from Joel's day to the invasion of Rome in AD 70, the time of the early Church.

Israel is still in dispersion today, although it is again a nation. The final bringing back of all the Jewish people will be supernatural, headed up by the Lord Jesus Himself. "He will send His angels with a great sound of a trumpet, and they will gather together His elect from the four winds" (Matthew 24:31).

Joel tells us now, the riches that were stolen from Jerusalem will be returned also. The plunder included the gold and silver, the goblets from Solomon's temple. Later, Belshazzar, the king of Babylon, called for these gold and silver utensils to use them to serve his guests at a large feast given in his own honor to celebrate his great glory and achievements. It was while he was eating and drinking from the sacred temple vessels that the handwriting of the Lord appeared on the wall, spelling out the king's doom. That very night Belshazzar was assassinated. The utensils were not like anything from other nations. They came from the temple of the living God and represented His divine presence with His people.

So it was with the Ark of the Covenant. It was not the Ark itself that was so important; it was the presence of the Lord that remained with it. When the enemies of the Lord stole the Ark, it brought a great curse on them. But whenever it was in the hands of the children of Israel, it brought great blessings to the people of Israel.

The Ark is lost today, but only from man. God knows exactly where it is, and even Indiana Jones doesn't know its location. But the presence of the Lord is not lost. God is still watching over Israel to bless her and to redeem her from her enemies. It is the same blessing and presence of the Lord with the Church. Jesus Himself told us, "I will never leave you nor forsake you" (Hebrews 13:5).

Now the Lord promises Israel He will restore their stolen possessions. He knows exactly where they are and how to bring all of it back to His temple in Jerusalem for His people—the descendants of Abraham, Isaac, and Jacob.

But perhaps the most important promise of all is that the people of Israel will be brought out of dispersion and captivity throughout the world and restored to their homeland once and for all. In the millennial reign of Jesus, Israel's dignity will be restored to her as the Lord fulfills all His unbreakable and eternal promises to them.

The Judgments of God

> 3:2 "I will also gather all nations, and bring them down to the Valley of Jehoshaphat; and I will enter into judgment with them there on account of My people, My heritage Israel, whom they have scattered among the nations; they have also divided up My land."

The Valley of Jehoshaphat literally means "Jehovah is Judge." To understand the full meaning of this title and what is about to take place in this Valley of Judgment, we must look at a moment before the Tribulation, at the time of the Rapture of the Church.

At this time of Jesus' coming for His saints, Christ will appear in the sky above the earth and will catch up all of the believers—those who are alive at the time, along with the resurrected dead in Christ. The entire Church will be together for the first time. They will enter into heaven with their Lord, where they will spend the next seven years with Him while earth is experiencing the Tribulation.

During this time the saints will be judged—not as to whether they enter into heaven, but to determine the extent of their rewards. The Greek does not call this the Judgment Seat, but rather the rewards seat of Christ. Believers from Pentecost to the Rapture will each stand before the Judgment Seat, or rewards seat, of Christ.

These rewards will be for the works or deeds done while on earth. If we did these works while spiritual, in fellowship with God, they are seen as gold, silver, and precious stones. If we did these works while carnal, out of fellowship with the

Lord, they are seen as wood, hay, and straw (1 Corinthians 3:10-15). All these works will be judged by fire, and those done while carnal—the wood, hay, and straw—will be burned up immediately. If we accomplished works while spiritual, in fellowship with God, they will not be burned up but rather even more purified. Fire cannot destroy gold, silver, and precious stones. After the fire, we will be rewarded for what is left over.

This is not a judgment to see if we go to heaven—that was settled at our salvation. This judgment is for our rewards in heaven for the works we did on earth after salvation. It is not a judgment for sinners, but for saints. This judgment in heaven will last seven years while the Tribulation is occurring on earth. The Judgment Seat of Christ will transform the Church into the bride of Christ.

At the end of the seven years of tribulation and the Judgment Seat of Christ occurring in heaven, Jesus will return with us to earth to reign with Him. And we will no longer be the Church, but the bride of Christ, returning to earth with Him.

Five Judgments

> "I will enter into judgment with them there [the nations who captured Israel] on account of My people, My heritage Israel, whom they have scattered among the nations; they have also divided up My people."

The first judgment by Jesus will be against the nations who have captured and enslaved Israel through the centuries. Jesus will gather the nations together who have tortured, murdered, and enslaved the Jewish people and stolen the treasures of their temple. His judgment against them will be declared that day.

The second judgment will occur after the battle of Armageddon is over. After the Lord has defeated the enemies of Israel and established His earthly kingdom, He will take the seat on His throne. This will be a judgment of the nations, separating believers from unbelievers—those saved during the Tribulation from those who were not (Matthew 25:31-46).

The third judgment will be of the believers who lived on earth during the Tribulation—those who were born again during that period of time and who remained true to the Lord despite the persecution by the antichrist and the satanic world religion. These "Tribulational saints" will then go into the millennial reign of the Lord Jesus.

The Church Age saints and those who died in the Tribulation will have resurrection bodies, while those who were saved during the Tribulation and survived will have natural bodies. Those who have natural bodies will have children during the Millennium, who will have to receive Jesus during the years that remain. Many will not receive Jesus and will one more time form a large army to rebel against Jesus—the ruler of earth, in a perfect environment and a curse-free earth. They will be immediately crushed by God's power as they come against Jesus' throne in Jerusalem (Revelation 20:7-10).

There will be a fourth judgment, which will occur after the Rapture of the Church (1 Thessalonians 4:16-17). It will take place at the beginning of the Millennium. Old Testament saints and sinners will be resurrected and judged by Christ.

The saints will resurrect to everlasting life; the sinners to eternal destruction (Daniel 12:1-2).

Finally, there will be a fifth and final judgment, which will occur at the end of the Millennium, the thousand-year reign of Christ on earth. A final rebellion of nations will be led by Satan, who will be released at the end of the Millennium. This will be the final proof that Satan cannot and will not change. God will crush this rebellion quickly, and everyone involved in it—Satan, fallen angels, demons, the antichrist, the false prophet, the beast, and all sinners who ever lived—will stand before God at the Great White Throne Judgment (Revelation 20:11-15). They will all be judged and sentenced to the lake of fire, eternal judgment.

The battle of Armageddon is really a judgment—one of several which will take place during the final days of the tribulation. God will gather the nations together in the Valley of Judgment for one final opportunity to receive Jesus as their Savior. When most refuse to do so, they seal their doom.

God's Case Against the Nations

> 3:3 "They have cast lots for My people, have given a boy as payment for a harlot, and sold a girl for wine, that they may drink."

"*They have cast lots for My people.*" This literally happened. In Obadiah 1:11, this is recorded against the nation of Edom: "In the day that you stood on the other side—in the day that strangers carried captive his forces, and foreigners entered his gates and cast lots for Jerusalem—even you were as one of them."

In the ancient world, a conquered people (especially the Jewish people) were nothing more than part of the spoils of war—something to be divided among the conquerors by gambling, by lots, and disposed of as they wished.

"And have given a boy for a harlot"—literally as a harlot. In those days, as in cases today, young boys were sold to homosexuals.

"And sold a girl for wine." Jewish girls were held in such low esteem by their enemies that they were sold into slavery and prostitution for the price of a glass of wine.

All these indicate how valueless the lives of God's people were in the eyes of their foes. No matter how moral the world may speak and act today, the feelings of hatred against Israel in most nations are still the same. These feelings are driven by Satan. But God's attitude toward Israel has never changed, despite their attitude toward Him. The nation of Israel is precious to the Lord. Nations today still want to destroy Israel, but Israel and Jerusalem will exist forever.

God's Recompense

The events of Joel 3:4-8 literally occurred in 2 Chronicles 21:16-17:

> Moreover the Lord stirred up against Jehoram the spirit of the Philistines and the Arabians who were near the Ethiopians. And they came up into Judah, and invaded it, and carried away all the possessions that were found in the king's house, and also his sons and his wives, so there was not a son left to him except Jehoahaz, the youngest of his sons.

The people of Joel's day remembered this event. It was still fresh in their memory. Joel reminds them of it because it illustrates the point God is about to make to them in the next five verses, in which He promises His people He is going to restore to them their possessions, their dignity, and their position. All these had been taken away from them by their enemies, but they will be restored to them. The Lord Himself will bring retribution to those who have wronged them in the past.

This passage, then, is meant to be a great comfort and joy to the people of Israel. When God declares He Himself is going to do something, it is no small matter. What God says He will do *will* come to pass! Our God never speaks lightly. He means what He says. He weighs very carefully every word that comes from His mouth, because once He has vowed to do something, the Lord has obligated Himself to Himself to see to it the words come to pass.

Now let's see what the Lord has promised He will do on behalf of His people Israel.

> 3:4-8 "Indeed, what have you to do with Me, O Tyre and Sidon, and all the coasts of Philisia? Will you retaliate against Me? But if you retaliate against Me, swiftly and speedily I will return your retaliation upon your own head; because you have taken My silver and My gold and have carried into your temples My prized possessions. Also the people of Judah and the people of Jerusalem you have sold to the Greeks, that you may remove them far from their borders. Behold I will raise them out of the place to which you have sold them and will return your retaliation upon your own

> head. I will sell your sons and your daughters into the hand of the people of Judah, and they will sell them to the Sabeans, to a people far off; for the Lord has spoken."

This charge against Tyre and Sidon is a warning to all the enemies who have come in and plundered and stolen from the house of Israel, God's chosen people.

"And all the coasts of Philistia? Will you retaliate against Me?" God is simply saying, "Don't you know when you attack My chosen ones, you attack Me? Do you really think you can *get even* with the Lord God of Israel?"

This should be a great object lesson for us today. When Satan comes against a child of God, he comes against God Himself. If you belong to the Lord, don't worry about protecting yourself. If you are standing on Scripture and your faith is in God, then God is your Defender, your Shield, and your Sword. The Lord God of Israel is your Fortress. He will fight for you in the day of battle. The battle is the Lord's. This is what the Lord is saying in this passage: "No one gets back at Me."

"But if you retaliate against Me, swiftly and speedily I will return your retaliation upon your own head." What the enemy does to God's people will fall back on their own heads. When Satan lays a trap for a child of God, he will fall into the trap himself. The arrows the devil launches at you and me will come back and strike him. When our enemies come at us from one direction, they will run in seven directions, because they are not attacking you and me—they are really attacking God! And no one ever gets the best of the Lord God of Israel!

Do you remember what the Lord told Abraham when He chose him as the one to be the father of His people Israel? "And I will bless those who bless you; and I will curse him who curses you; and in you all the families of the earth shall be blessed" (Genesis 12:3). Make no mistake about it, God defends His own. Beside the Word of God, human history bears out this truth. The rise and fall of most nations have been attributed to the way they treated the Jewish people.

Nations do not go under for no reason. There are spiritual reasons why many nations succeed or fall. And foremost among these reasons is the nation's supply of salt—dedicated, praying disciples of the Lord, the "salt of the earth." Another spiritual resource that creates protection for a nation are the Christians who look to their spiritual heritage, Israel. We are seen as the "seed of Abraham" from the moment we are born again. Paul reminds us that Abraham is the father of us all—Jew and Gentile (Romans 4:16). Our attitude as Christians toward the nation of Israel is one of the determining factors in our own country's strength and success. What happens in Israel and Jerusalem should be far more important than what happens in the United States. When Jesus comes back to rule, He will not touch down in Washington, DC.

"Because you have carried into your temples My prized possessions. Also the people of Judah and the people of Jerusalem you have sold to the Greeks, that you may remove them far from their borders." This event really took place. Tyre and Sidon sold the children of Israel into slavery in Greece for profit. As a result, Tyre and Sidon came under a curse. Jesus even mentioned this fact hundreds of years later when He said of certain cities, "It will be more tolerable for Tyre and Sidon at the day of judgment than for you" (Matthew 11:22).

Because of their guilt, in verse 8 the Lord says to the enemies of Israel: "I will sell your sons and your daughters into the hand of the people of Judah, and they will sell them to the Sabeans, to a people far off." The nation of Sabea was located at the southern tip of Arabia—about as far away as a person could travel from Israel in the days of the ancient world. This is where the Queen of Sheba traveled from to visit Solomon. The Bible says she came "from the uttermost parts of the earth" (Matthew 12:42 KJV).

"*For the Lord has spoken.*" Can there possibly be any doubt, then, that this prophetic judgment will fall on the enemies of Israel? Is there anything in this world as sure as that which "the Lord has spoken"? God will have His recompense on His enemies.

GOD'S DECLARATION OF WAR

> 3:9 "Proclaim this among the nations: "Prepare for war! Wake up the mighty men, let all the men of war draw near, let them come up."

"Proclaim this among the Gentiles: 'Prepare for war!'" This again refers to the battle of Armageddon. The Lord is speaking to all the Gentile nations, declaring war against them.

"Wake up the mighty men; let all the men draw near." The "mighty men" is a reference to the warriors—the professional soldiers, the most skilled and expert fighting men. "All the men" refers to the rank and file, the enlisted soldiers, many called back from civilian life, who go to add their strength to the army.

Here the Lord is taunting the Gentile nations of the world to come to battle with Him. All the armies of the earth are challenged to ally themselves together and make war against the Lord God of Hosts: "Hear ye, hear ye! Jehovah is taking on all comers!" The Lord has finally come to the point where He is "spoiling for a fight"! And He knows what the final outcome will be.

And so do we. We know the battle of Armageddon is going to be won by the Lord. And He is not going to have to raise so much as a finger to do it. The words of His mouth will slay all the mighty men of war arrayed together against Him. Out of His mouth will come a sharp two-edged sword, and with it He will defend Israel and take vengeance on all those who have persecuted and abused His people, Israel, throughout their history.

You and I, during the Church Age, are living in the day of grace—in the day of God's long-suffering and patience. We believers have not been appointed to wrath, but to "obtain salvation through our Lord Jesus Christ" (1 Thessalonians 5:9). But there is coming a day when those who have rejected God's grace will have to face His judgment and wrath. And when this happens, their fate is sealed forever.

> 3:10 "Beat your plowshares into swords and your pruning hooks into spears; let the weak say, 'I am strong.'"

"Beat your plowshares into swords, and your pruning hooks into spears." A plowshare was used in ancient times to break up the fields for planting. There are a few in our day who still use this method, but most of it today is mechanized. A pruning hook was for cutting back the branches of trees in an orchard to make them bear more fruit. Here the Lord is telling His enemies to beat their plowshares into swords and their pruning hooks into spears in preparation for battle against God.

To do this shows desperation to defend yourself and your family. What would normally help to feed you has to be beaten into a weapon to kill an approaching army. Preservation is now more important than food for the family. All nations of the world will be gearing up for war. Normal peacetime production will be halted, and emphasis will be shifted to the production of armaments. The workforce will no longer be engaged in turning out consumer goods and services, but will labor around the clock to produce weapons of destruction for their enemies and for the self-preservation of their families.

Just ask about our own nation in the 1940s when America had to abruptly switch from peacetime production to wartime output after the outbreak of World War II. The last days before the battle of Armageddon will be a time of unprecedented military buildup throughout the world.

In Isaiah 2:3-4 we find an interesting parallel to our story in Joel:

> ...Come and let us go up to the mountain of the Lord, to the house of the God of Jacob; He will teach us His ways, and we shall walk in His paths. For out of Zion shall go forth the law, and the word of the Lord from Jerusalem. He shall judge between the nations and rebuke many people; they shall beat their swords into plowshares, and their spears into pruning hooks. Nation shall not lift up sword against nation, neither shall they learn war anymore.

The verses in Joel do not contradict the verses in Isaiah. Joel tells the people to prepare for war, and Isaiah tells the people the war is over. Each author stands on different sides of the battle of Armageddon. Joel sees the battle coming and the people are to prepare for it. Isaiah sees the victory of Jesus at the battle and the great peace which comes after the battle. No human being or human weapon will win at Armageddon—Jesus Christ will win. He judges between the nations and brings the victory. Now the national economy can return to plowing, planting, and harvesting crops. After Armageddon, there will be no more defense budgets: "Neither shall they learn war anymore."

Joel's command to the armies in verse 10 is, "Let the weak say, 'I am strong.'" This is a challenge by God to His enemies to stand on their own two feet and get ready to do battle with Him.

Armageddon is the last battle where people will go to war. At the end of the Millennium, armies will form and ally with Satan to fight Jesus. These are unbelievers born during the Millennium who will rebel against perfect leadership, a perfect world government, and a perfect environment of clean water, air, and food. Even in a perfect environment, the issue will be accepting or rejecting Jesus Christ. Mankind's problem is not environment, the problem is their heart of rebellion toward God and His plan of salvation.

An army as large as the one at Armageddon will be formed, and Satan will be loosed for a short season to round up the rebels to fight Jesus. But this battle will not even be fought. No weapons will have to be made to fight. This gigantic army of those who despise God and righteousness will surround Jerusalem to destroy it—but heaven will open and fire will come down from God the Father and devour them in a split second.

After this, the Great White Throne Judgment will take place, and Satan will be cast into the lake of fire. All who supported his cause will join him. "They will be tormented day and night forever and ever" (Revelation 20:10).

9

GOD'S ETERNAL GLORY

JOEL 3:11-21

GOD SITS IN JUDGMENT

> 3:11 "Assemble and come, all you nations, and gather together all around. Cause Your mighty ones to go down there, O Lord."

"Assemble and come, all you nations." The word *heathen* refers to Gentiles. Throughout the New Testament these two words are almost interchangeable. It is the Greek word *ethna,* from which we get our English word *ethnic.* When God speaks of the heathen, it is a reference to all the Gentile nations He is inviting to come and make war against Israel.

"And gather together all around. Cause Your mighty ones go down there, O Lord." Joel is giving the attacking nations God's invitation to the Valley of Jehoshaphat, or Valley of

Judgment. What looks like a simple victory to the armies of the nations will be the quickest and most powerful battle they have ever been through. They will be defeated quickly and decisively. They will not be defeated by Israel, but by Israel's God—the Lord Jesus, in battle array.

> 3:12 "Let the nations be wakened and come up to the Valley of Jehoshaphat; for there I will sit to judge all the surrounding nations."

"For there I will sit to judge all the nations." We are now approaching the end. After thousands of years, judgment is about to be pronounced on the enemies of God and His people, Israel. We have already learned of the Valley of Jehoshaphat, the Valley of Decision. This is the place where those who are attacking Jerusalem will be held in supernatural darkness for 24 hours. This is the last opportunity for the lost to be saved. This is also the time when Jesus will break the intense darkness with His return, "as lightning that comes from the east and is visible even in the west" (Matthew 24:27 NIV).

> 3:13 "Put in the sickle for the harvest is ripe. Come, go down; for the winepress is full, the vats overflow—for their wickedness is great."

This verse relates to Joel 2:23, where the Lord referred to the latter rain and the harvesting of crops. As we studied before, the former rain is the glory of God manifested in the Old Testament. The latter rain is God's glory in the New Testament. We have seen that in the Millennium the Lord will bring together the glory of both the Old and the New Testaments. In other words, the saints of the Old Testament and those of the New Testament will all be gathered together and will all enter the millennial reign of the Lord.

The glory that was revealed to Abraham, that shone on the face of Moses, that was present in the pillar of fire by night and the cloud by day, the glory that filled the wilderness tabernacle and the temple of Solomon—will be combined with the glory that was manifested on the Day of Pentecost and which has been poured out now for more than 2,000 years. All of this combined glory, the former and the latter rain, will be united in the very first month of the earthly reign of the Lord Jesus.

Joel 2:24 then told us the floors will be full of wheat, and the vats will overflow with wine and oil. This means that in the Millennium, the Spirit of the Lord and His prosperity will be poured out to overflowing. Every believer—every person on earth—will be filled, baptized with the Holy Spirit, the manifested glory of God.

Let's compare these two verses from Joel chapter 2 with this verse from Joel chapter 3, which also speaks of overflowing vats. There is a marked difference between them. In Joel 2, the vats were a symbol of the blessings of the Lord. The vats of Joel 3 are of the wickedness of fallen mankind meeting God's judgment. But this judgment will be poured out only on those who have rejected the Lord. It is reserved for God's enemies. They are the ones whom the Lord will baptize with fire (Matthew 3:11).

But just as the wickedness of man and God's judgment will overflow on that day upon His enemies, so will God's grace then be poured out in greater abundance on those who have put their trust in Him. "Where sin abounded, grace abounded much more" (Romans 5:20). The Lord will demonstrate His judgment on the heathen nations in the Valley of Judgment, but it will be only a short time before He will pour out His glory—the former and latter rain—on the redeemed throughout the Millennium.

The Sickle of the Lord

"Put in the sickle, for the harvest is ripe." In Matthew 13 we read about this sickle in harvest time as a symbol of gathering souls. The chapter gives seven parables, which we call the Kingdom Parables. In these seven parables Jesus describes the Church Age, which was about to come, and the Tribulation.

The first of these parables is about the sower and the seed (Matthew 13:3-9). The sower is the believer, and the seed is the Word of God. By this the Lord was illustrating how those who believe in Him are to go throughout the nations of the world (the field), sowing the seed of God's Word and spreading the gospel. The same seed can both save the sinner and disciple the believer.

Later, after this parable, Jesus gave another parable describing a different sower and seed in Matthew 13:24-30. This is an end-time parable describing the close of the Tribulation and the separating of those who reject the gospel—sinners—from those who accept the gospel—believers. Those who accept the gospel will go into the millennial reign of Jesus. Those who reject the gospel will be sent to hell. The ones who accept the gospel are called *wheat*. The ones who reject Jesus and salvation are called *tares*. Tares look like wheat but have no value or use and can only be separated and burned.

> Another parable He put forth to them, saying: "The kingdom of heaven is like a man who sowed good seed in his field; but while men slept, his enemy came and sowed tares among the wheat and went his way. But when the grain had sprouted and produced a crop, then the tares also appeared. So the servants of the owner came and said to him, 'Sir, did you not sow good seed in your field? How then does it have tares?' He said to them, 'An enemy has done this.' The servants said to him, 'Do you want us then to go and gather them up?' But he said, 'No, lest while you gather up the tares you also uproot the wheat with them. Let both grow together until the harvest, and at the time of harvest I will say to the reapers: "First gather together the tares and bind them in bundles to burn them but gather the wheat into my barn"'" (Matthew 13:24-31).

What does this have to do with our passage in Joel? Our job as servants of God is to make converts out of sinners and disciples out of converts. It is not up to us to change the world or rid it of sin, but to fulfill the two parts of the Great Commission—giving the gospel to the sinner and discipling the new converts. Jesus will handle the world, separating wheat from tares, believers from unbelievers. He will not do our job of witnessing and making disciples, and we cannot do His job of purifying the world.

I am not saying we do not get concerned or involved with the problems of society, but we know the answer is not which individual or party is in charge, but rather a renewed urgency to wake up believers and get back to what will ultimately change a nation: the new birth, scriptural understanding, and application.

Purifying the world will be handled by the angels, first as they separate the believers from the unbelievers. This will be done at Jesus' coming at the end of the Tribulation to set up His kingdom. After the angels separate the wheat (believers saved during the Tribulation) from the tares (unbelievers), He will judge the tares by sentencing them to hell to await the Great White Throne Judgment and the eternal lake of fire. Jesus will then take the wheat (believers) with Him into the barns—His millennial kingdom and eternal reign.

In our text Joel is saying in verse 13: *"Put in the sickle, for the harvest is ripe."* The ones who will put in the sickle are the angels who will be coming back to earth with Jesus (Matthew 13:41). This harvest is not the kind we usually think of—natural seed and tares—but the gathering of believers and unbelievers for judgment, a harvest of all earth's inhabitants. Some will go into the kingdom of their Father, others into eternal punishment. If a person has not received Jesus by the time of His return to reign eternally on earth, it will be too late. God's patience will have been exhausted.

The Valley of Decision

> 3:14 "Multitudes, multitudes in the valley of decision! For the day of the Lord is near in the valley of decision."

Some time ago, I was in the Holy Land and visited the Valley of Armageddon. What a moving experience it was to stand and look across this largest valley in the world and realize that one day all the armies of the nations of the earth will be gathered there in one huge military maneuver against the tiny nation of Israel. From that vantage point on the heights outside Jerusalem, it is plain to see that there is only one way to enter the valley—from the north. As I stood there, remembering these verses from Joel, I could picture all those armies descending on Jerusalem to surround and destroy God's chosen people.

But I also recalled that there is going to come another army that day—this one from the sky—as heaven opens up like a scroll and the Lord Jesus comes with battalions of saints and angels.

Angels have fought human beings before and always won. Their power could destroy the armies coming in, but they won't get to fight this battle. Jesus will only open His mouth, and the Word of God will come out as a sharp two-edged sword to destroy the nations about to attack His chosen nation and people, Israel. One Man will destroy millions of military men with His voice.

> 3:15 "The sun and moon will grow dark, and the stars will diminish their brightness."

The sun, moon, and stars will all go dark. Just preceding the return of the Lord, the sun and moon will be darkened, and the stars will refuse to shine. For 24 hours, time itself will seem to hang suspended. During this period, the people of the world will not be able to see anything. The darkness covering the whole earth will be so intense that no man-made light will be able to penetrate or subdue it. Flashlights, headlights, and searchlights will be useless. No natural light will penetrate supernatural darkness.

This is the same type of darkness that covered the earth while Jesus was on the Cross.

Throughout those long hours, all creation will lie in black, dark stillness. There will be nothing to do but meditate and think. This is the Valley of Decision. The fate of the world will hang in the balance as the Lord holds back His judgment to give the nations one final chance to repent, turn to Him, and be saved.

At the end of the 24 hours, Jesus will return as lightning, and every eye will see Him, and every tongue will confess He is Lord (Philippians 2:10-11). But for those who continue to reject Him, it will be too late.

THE LORD RETURNS

> 3:16 "The Lord also will roar from Zion, and utter His voice from Jerusalem; the heavens and earth will shake; but the Lord will be a shelter for His people, and the strength of the children of Israel."

"The Lord also will roar from Zion." Suddenly, the stillness will be shattered as the Lord comes roaring out of heaven to rescue His people and bring final judgment on His enemies who have refused His grace and forgiveness. He will appear as lightning from the east to the west. Just as the earth was in 24 hours of darkness, now it will have 24 hours of light, as the whole earth will see the glory of the coming of the Lord. Zechariah tells us about that day:

> It shall come to pass in that day, that there will be no light; the lights will diminish. It shall be one day which is known to the Lord—neither day nor night. But at evening time it shall happen that it will be light (Zechariah 14:6-7).

The same intensity of darkness will be spread over the entire earth. One side of the earth will not be experiencing night while the other side experiences day. The earth will be dark everywhere until Jesus appears. He will come through the darkness and bring God's glory—divine, supernatural light. Then there will be no darkness, only light worldwide. God's light is different from nature's light or man's light. When God's glory appears at Jesus' coming, removing the darkness, there will be no shadows on the earth. Like heaven, light will appear from all directions. This is God's light compared to nature's light or man's light. John spoke of this time yet to come in Revelation:

> And the kings of the earth, the great men, the rich men, the commanders, the mighty men, every slave and every free man, hid themselves in the caves and in the rocks of the mountains, and said to the mountains and rocks, "Fall on us and hide us from the face of Him who sits on the throne, and from the wrath of the Lamb! For the great day of His wrath has come, and who shall be able to stand?" (Revelation 6:15-17)

The enemies of the Lord—those who have rejected Him—will flee from the light, trying to find release through suicide. But since death will be removed, no one will be able to escape their judgment. One by one, they will have to stand before Jesus on that day and face Him as the ultimate Judge over the whole earth.

"And the heavens and the earth will shake." There is going to be an earthquake on the day the Lord returns. This earthquake is mentioned many times in the Bible—Joel 2:10; Zechariah 14:4; Isaiah 13:13; Jeremiah 10:10; Matthew 24:29; Luke 21:25-27. The earthquake will be so intense it will cause the Mount of Olives to split down the middle, releasing a river of water that will travel to the Mediterranean Sea.

"But the Lord will be the hope of His people and the strength of the children of Israel." Notice the wording: the hope of His people and the strength of the children of Israel. God's people are not only the children of Israel, but Gentile believers as well.

It has been noted several times that the Tribulation will be a great time of evangelism throughout the world. At the end of the Tribulation, when the Lord returns to earth, He is going to spare the believing Gentiles on earth just as He will spare the believing Jews. This is because, as believers, we are neither Jew nor Gentile. In Christ, our physical nationality means nothing. It is faith from the heart toward the work of Jesus that makes us part of God's family.

God's angels will be sent to gather not only the Jews who have accepted the Lord during the Tribulation but also the Gentiles who have believed on Him. It will not be exclusively the children of Israel rescued on that day, but all who have trusted in Jesus for salvation and are looking for their Lord's return.

When the end comes, the Lord will send out His angels to harvest believers and unbelievers, wheat and tares alike.

When the sickle of the Lord is put in, both Jewish and Gentile believers will be gathered into the Kingdom. But all unbelievers from all nations, like the tares, will be destroyed with unquenchable fire.

> 3:17 "So you shall know that I am the Lord your God, dwelling in Zion My holy mountain. Then Jerusalem shall be holy, and no aliens shall ever pass through her again."

What the New Heavens and Earth Will Be Like

Joel 3:17 introduces the Millennium and the eternal kingdom from the viewpoint of Jesus' headquarters—Jerusalem. You cannot get away from the importance of Israel and Jerusalem. The United States, Europe, and other nations are the beneficiaries of the blessings poured out on Israel, not the center of them. Jesus will rule from Jerusalem throughout the 1,000 years of His reign, and then forever, after the Millennium, into the time of His eternal kingdom.

This will be after the final rebellion at the end of the Millennium. The Great White Throne Judgment will occur between the end of the Millennium and the beginning of the New Heaven and Earth. This will be the judgment of all sinners who have ever lived—and of Satan, demons, fallen angels, the antichrist, the false prophet, and the beast. They will all be cast eternally into the lake of fire.

The complete restoration of the earth will occur, along with the removal of all remembrances of evil, man's empires, and human rule. All things will be made new. The renovated earth will be ruled by Jesus Christ, who will sit on His throne in Jerusalem forever. There will be no more rebellions—only perfect peace forever, coming from the rulership of the Prince of Peace.

All people on earth will have resurrection bodies, and Heaven will come down and rest over Jerusalem. Heaven will then be called the New Jerusalem. Jerusalem has no recorded beginning and no end—it is truly the eternal city. This is all recorded in the last two chapters of the Bible, Revelation 20 and 21.

All believers who have ever lived on earth will have resurrection bodies. These bodies are unique. They require no food but can eat. Jesus ate with His disciples after His resurrection. They can breathe, but do not need to. With a resurrection body, Jesus breathed on His disciples so the Holy Spirit could dwell in them before He departed. The resurrection body can disappear and reappear at will, walk through walls, and be touched and handled. Jesus did all these things after His resurrection.

And an even more incredible accomplishment can be made—a resurrection body can travel through space, disappear, and reappear at any destination at the speed of thought. Just think of a place, and you can be there. Angels do this. They can disappear from heaven and instantly appear on earth to deliver us from any situation without the passage of time being involved. Jesus rose from the Mount of Olives slowly, but He probably arrived instantly in heaven when He disappeared from the sight of the disciples.

We will be able to do this in our future resurrection bodies. We can visit any planet, galaxy, or star system at the speed of thought. Just think it—and you will be there.

This is far greater than the speed of light, because in a resurrection body all distances take the same amount of time—instantaneous.

You will probably be able to live anywhere on earth you want. Every country and city will have perfect weather with no night. The entire earth will be lit by the glory of God from Jerusalem. There will be no need for sleep—resurrection bodies do not sleep.

The city of Jerusalem will be visited annually by all people from all nations as a remembrance of the cost it took to bring them to this point—the sacrifice of Jesus. The occasion will be the last feast God instituted, the Feast of Tabernacles. It celebrates that Jesus will live, or *tabernacle*, with us forever. All the feasts have been fulfilled, but this one will be celebrated annually on the new earth.

If you know this is your future, why do you fear today? If you are saved, born again, and have given your life entirely to Jesus, this is your future—guaranteed. Satan's future is also guaranteed. The one who is harassing and tempting you will spend 1,000 years in hell after Jesus returns. He will then spend eternity in the lake of fire. He will never be released, and he cannot escape.

You have the future he wanted but can never have. The next time Satan tempts you to leave the plan of God and follow him, remind him: "Satan, I read the end of the Book. I win, and you lose. Go bother someone who doesn't know that."

Prosperity Flows

> 3:18 "And it will come to pass in that day that the mountains shall drip with new wine, the hills shall flow

> with milk, and all the brooks of Judah shall be flooded with water; a fountain shall flow from the house of the Lord and water the Valley of Acacias."

"The mountains shall drip with new wine, and the hills shall flow with milk." In the symbolic language of Joel's day, this was a picture of great prosperity. After Armageddon is over, all sinners have been removed, and the Millennium begins, overflowing prosperity will be given to the inhabitants of all nations. Where will these riches come from?

The answer is found in Zechariah 14:14: "Judah also will fight at Jerusalem; and the wealth of all the surrounding nations shall be gathered together—gold, silver, and apparel in great abundance." This verse should remind us of another familiar scripture in Proverbs 13:22: "...the wealth of the sinner is stored up for the righteous." This verse is speaking of the time Jesus returns to earth to rule. It also has an application found throughout the Word of God and includes believers today. People may steal from you, but God can and will make it up to you.

After the invasion of one army of five allied wicked kings, Abraham rode off to battle to recover his nephew Lot and his family who had been taken captive. He came back with Lot and his family, and also all who had been taken (Genesis 14:16). He also returned with much treasure from the wicked king and gave tithes from it to Melchisedec, the priest.

Also, David and his army of men camped in Ziklag. They returned one day to find their wives, children, and goods stolen by the Amalekites. David led his men into battle, and they rescued their families and brought back a great amount of treasure to the camp. David's own men argued over who was entitled to the goods, and David told them, "As his part is who goes down to the battle, so shall his part be who stays by the supplies; they shall share alike" (1 Samuel 30:24). David took his portion of the treasure, got on his horse, and took great amounts of money back to the kings who had hidden him from Saul during the time Saul tried to kill David.

Both Abraham and David knew the treasures came from God, and we have an obligation—out of love for God—to give a portion to those in need. God does not give us blessings in life to hoard. We will leave them here when we die anyway. He always gives extra to us to be a financial blessing to those preaching the gospel and to the poor in need. He never gives it to us to hold back from others and spend it only on ourselves.

Jacob is another great example. When he was taken advantage of by his father-in-law, who kept back money from Jacob ten times, Jacob remained faithful in his work and received the woman he desired. Though he was cheated, Jacob kept his trust in God and died a wealthy man.

God has never been against prosperity; He is against greed. "...no good thing will He withhold from those who walk uprightly" (Psalm 84:11).

THE LAND IS HEALED

"And all the rivers of Judah shall flow with waters" (KJV). These waters are healing waters. From Zechariah we learn that on the day the Lord returns, His feet will touch down on the Mount of Olives, which will split in two in the middle, and floods of water will come out of it (Zechariah 14:4-8).

Ezekiel tells us more: "This water flows toward the eastern region, goes down into the valley, and enters the sea. When it reaches the sea, its waters are healed. And it shall be that everything that moves, wherever the rivers go, will live. ...for they will be healed, and everything will live wherever the river goes" (Ezekiel 47:8-9).

Verse 10 goes on to say the water will even heal the Dead Sea. Today, nothing lives in the Dead Sea. But on that day, "It shall be that fishermen will stand by it from En Gedi to En Eglaim; they will be places for spreading their nets. Their fish will be of the same kinds as the fish of the Great Sea, exceedingly many" (Ezekiel 47:10). These two small towns will be fishing villages on the Dead Sea one day.

When God heals, it always brings a blessing.

Enemies Are Cursed

> 3:19 "Egypt shall be a desolation, and Edom a desolate wilderness, because of violence against the people of Judah, for they have shed innocent blood in their land."

Joel says the only curses pronounced at that time will be against the nations who have shed the innocent blood of God's people. Two nations are named that specifically came against Israel for no reason but simply to plunder and enslave the Jewish people—Egypt and Edom (Syria). Because Egypt and Syria have held the children of Israel in bondage in the past, God's wrath will be poured out on them. They will be cursed before the blessing of the Lord is poured out on the whole earth.

THE LORD GOD OMNIPOTENT REIGNS

> 3:20 "But Judah shall abide forever, and Jerusalem from generation to generation."

I have stated from both the Old and New Testaments that Jerusalem is the eternal city. It has been before, and will be again, the capital for the rulership of Jesus Christ. When He returns after Armageddon, He will rule from Jerusalem forever.

In the meantime, Israel has always been protected by God. Other nations have conquered the city, but none have possessed it for long. The Jews have returned each time. The longest period Israel has been inhabited by other nations has been during the Church Age—from the destruction of the temple by Rome until the end of the Tribulation.

> 3:21 "For I will acquit them of the guilt of bloodshed, whom I had not acquitted; for the Lord dwells in Zion."

To "acquit the guilt of bloodshed" is God avenging the blood of the Jews shed throughout their existence. There is still an amount of cleansing to be done, and God never forgets to keep the promises He has made to His people. God is simply saying, "I have not forgotten what I said to you."

Through the prophet Jeremiah, the Lord spoke comfort to Israel during their time of captivity in Babylon. He assured them: "For I know the thoughts that I think toward you, says the Lord, thoughts of peace and not of evil, to give you a future and a hope [expectation]" (Jeremiah 29:11).

God never forgot the promises made to His people Israel, and He will not forget those He has made to us. He may not fulfill the promises in the amount of time you desire, but He always settles them. He cannot forget.

Let's end our study of Joel's book with a promise given to us from Revelation. A multitude in heaven is shouting out to us not to give up—God keeps His Word:

> ...Alleluia! Salvation and glory and honor and power belong to the Lord our God! For true and righteous are His judgments, because He has judged the great harlot who corrupted the earth with her fornication, and He has avenged on her the blood of His servants shed by her (Revelation 19:1-2).

If God has kept all His promises to the saints who have gone on to heaven and writes in Revelation that He will keep His Word to us to destroy false religions and sin yet to come, then we can give Him glory today for His faithfulness in the past and His faithfulness yet to come.

God does not give greater respect to anyone. He loves each of us as much as He loves Abraham, Moses, David, Elijah, and Jesus Himself.

I'll see you in heaven.

ABOUT BOB YANDIAN

BOB YANDIAN pastored Grace Church in Tulsa, Oklahoma, for 33 years. In 2013, he began a new phase of ministry and passed the pastoral baton to his son, Robb. Bob's mission is to train up a new generation in the Word of God through his "Student of the Word" broadcast and by ministering at Bible schools, ministers' conferences, and churches. Bob is a graduate of Trinity Bible College and has served as instructor and Dean of Instructors at RHEMA Bible Training Center. Called a "pastor's pastor," Bob established the School of the Local Church that has trained and sent hundreds of ministers to churches and missions organizations around the world.